THE CHORD FACTORY

BUILD YOUR OWN GUITAR CHORD DICTIONARY

WRITTEN AND ILLUSTRATED
BY JON DAMIAN

EDITED BY JONATHAN FEIST

Berklee Press

Vice President: David Kusek
Dean of Continuing Education: Debbie Cavalier
Managing Editor: Jonathan Feist
Director of Business Affairs: Robert F. Green
Senior Designer: Robert Heath
Editorial Assistants: Rajasri Mallikarjuna, James Speight, Jonathan Whalen

ISBN-13: 978-0-87639-075-7
ISBN-10: 0-87639-075-0

DISTRIBUTED BY

HAL•LEONARD®
CORPORATION
7777 W. BLUEMOUND RD. P.O. BOX 13819
MILWAUKEE, WISCONSIN 53213

1140 Boylston Street
Boston, MA 02215-3693 USA
(617) 747-2146

Visit Berklee Press Online at
www.berkleepress.com

Visit Hal Leonard Online at
www.halleonard.com

TABLE OF CONTENTS

PREFACE

As with my first book, *The Guitarist's Guide to Composing and Improvising*, this present volume, *The Chord Factory*, is a reflection of my curiosity as a student of the guitar. In both volumes, I share years of study and exploration with this most fascinating of instruments. The creative process behind *The Chord Factory* is based upon my own curiosity in chord exploration. I invite you to join in this building process as you develop your own guitar chord dictionary.

Observe chords as actors on your musical stage, each with a distinct personality. Gradually, through the chord-building process, you will understand these harmonic characters and the fascinating and endless possibilities they offer to your musical world.

Good luck!

ACKNOWLEDGMENTS

Thanks to my family—Betsy, Ben, and Gene—for their loving support; to Jonathan Feist at Berklee Press for editorial and Finale support; to Debbie Cavalier at Berklee Media for publishing support; to Larry Baione, Rick Peckham, and Matt Marvuglio at Berklee College for leadership support; to Simon Winchester for his book's inspirational support; to Laura my yoga teacher for inversional support; to Ralph Rosen for Beatles and Pygmy research; to Joel Press for historical support; to Juliana Horton for CrossTones Puzzle and inverting support; to Joe Mulholland for altered support; to Jon Voigt for tune research support; and to Madeleine Toh for software support.... Oh, and thanks to my brother Butch for stopping his trumpet lessons!

This building project needed a lot of support!

It sure did, Chester, and thank you for your support too!

INTRODUCTION: A PRE-CONSTRUCTION MEETING

Several years ago, I built my own guitar chord dictionary. I built it not only for my curious self but also to help my early-level students grasp the inner workings of the fascinating world of guitar chords. I also built it out of frustration with the status quo of chord books in which one sees a pretty picture of a chord form but never learns how it is related to all the other pretty chord forms.

In the construction process—and this is after more than forty years of banging on the gitbox (guitar)—I learned so many new chord forms and ideas. I realized that all levels of guitarists should try building their own dictionaries, from the bottom up. Hence, this book.

I will guide you through the step-by-step process of building your own chord dictionary from the ground up. From this experience, you will gain a deeper understanding of chords and harmony.

This project is for all levels of chord explorers, from professional-level guitarists in need of harmonic stimulation or to fill in some "gray areas," to the early guitarist just embarking on that fascinating and fun aspect of exploring chords and harmony. This added chord vocabulary will strengthen all areas of your musical world as a performer and composer.

You can join fully in the construction process, or simply enjoy the text and examples as a harmonic treatise, or do some of each. The choice is yours.

Searching for the bigger, better, cooler-than-the-last-chord-I-found chord has always been fun for me, as a guitarist. I can still remember running around the house showing off the first C Major 7 chord I learned. It was, and still is, beautiful! That pretty, open-string chord form was easy to play for a new guitar player. And my mom Rosie smiled patiently as I strummed my newfound treasure. And yikes! Forty years later, the search continues!

I also learned that bigger is not always better. In fact, that's why I start our building project with 1-note chords!

Say Jon, that's a pretty small chord, one note?!

You're right, Chester!

Folks, allow me to introduce my buddy Chester. He will help us build our dictionary.

Yes, Chester, it is a small chord. Consider, though, that in a standard dictionary, words like that cute little article "a" and that very personal pronoun "I" are easily more important than those spelling-bee busters "perineurium" or "flocculent." Similarly, the smaller chord forms are what larger chord forms are built from.

"Working from the bottom up" will help us understand relationships between chords and how and why they act as they do.

One of the most fun things about exploring chords, for me, is to actually play and experience them firsthand. With this in mind, I have fully illustrated this book with clear chord templates to introduce chord ideas and help you play them, hear them, and put them into action—to create that personal interaction and sense of discovery with chords that I will always enjoy. Playing the examples that accompany the text is a most important part of the book since they act as a hands-on "score" for the book. Play these examples, touch them, hear them.

This book simply portrays my process for constructing my own dictionary. You are welcome to join me. You don't have to take breaks when I do. Set your own pace. There is the "Break" chapter, in which you can try some games, like the "The Chord Symbols CrossTones Puzzle" or "The Incredible Time-Machine Study." As you will see, most tools will be provided. Only a sharp pencil, an eraser, curiosity, hard work, and your guitar are needed to start building on your own dictionary. Which, by the way, will never be completed.

This is a good thing. In fact, you will unearth chord forms that I haven't found yet. Send them to me. Most importantly, have fun, and always wear your hard hat for protection.

> Warning! In the construction process, you will encounter challenging stretches for your chording hand. *Do not hurt yourself.* Know your physical limits, which will change with time. This hand warning icon will be shown occasionally throughout the construction process as an important reminder.

I do it as a safety measure. In fact, in the Break Room chapter (chapter 12), there are some hand and arm stretches I learned in yoga class. They have really helped me to get warmed up and also to avoid injuries from playing some of these chords!

GETTING AROUND

Note: This Introduction will be using music language words such as "3rd degree" or chord symbols not introduced yet. These terms will be gradually and clearly explained as construction begins in chapter 1.

THE LANGUAGES USED DURING CONSTRUCTION

In this construction process, several "languages" will be used. They will help in constructing and understanding the architecture behind the building process. The languages used are the Chord Template Language, the Standard Music Notation Language, the Tablature Language, the Chord Symbol Language, and the Interval Language. Here is a brief look at each of them.

The Chord Template Language

The Chord Template Language is the main language used throughout construction. The chord templates used here show what the chord form looks like as you peek over the fingerboard, down at your chording hand.

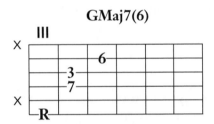

Fig. I.1. GMaj7(6) Template

In this template, the bottom line is that big, fat, low E string that's closest to your nose. The top line is that skinny E string farthest from your nose. Numbers and letters indicate where to place your fingers and also indicate each degree of the chord, labeled to give you a theoretical view of the chord's makeup. The letter **R** represents the root of the chord. Numbers indicate chord degrees. For example, in figure I.1, the number **3** indicates the major 3rd degree of the GMaj7(6) chord.

Some template examples indicate a particular position to be used for a chord fingering. The Roman numeral indicates what fret the chord is built on. In figure I.1, the Roman numeral **III** indicates the 3rd fret. If instead of a Roman numeral you see an infinity symbol (∞), the fingering can be played in any position; set a specific root as needed. An x to the left of a template indicates that a string is not played or deadened (muted). These strings are muted generally with the help of a chording hand finger that rests gently on the string to be deadened. If you see a degree number or letter to the left of the template instead of an x, play an open string for that chord degree.

Here is another fingering for a GMaj7(6), this time using open strings. Here, the G, B, and high E open strings are indicated to the left of the template with respective chord degrees: the root, 3rd, and 6th degrees of GMaj7(6).

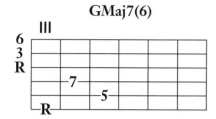

Fig. I.2. GMaj7(6) Open-String Form

Those open strings sound sweet on that chord, Jon.

They add a nice bright sound to the chord, Chester.

In chapter 2, "Dyads: 2-Part Chords," ovals (O) indicate where to place your fingers, as specific degrees are not necessary in describing simple 2-part chords (intervals).

Repeat signs indicate that an example is a vamp and should be repeated several times to help work on chord shifting with a rhythmic groove of your choice. Barlines indicate measures.

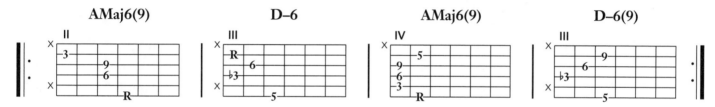

Fig. I.3. Repeat Signs

The Blank Template

There is a blank template sheet on figure 14.1 of the "Tool Box" chapter (chapter 14). You will need to photocopy a pile of these to build your dictionary. There are forty templates on each template page, four columns by ten rows. For future reference, let's agree on a numbering scheme for them. Let's call the first template, in the upper left-hand corner of the sheet, template 1, and reading left to right and down brings us to the last template in the bottom right-hand corner, template 40! So template 16 is where? Right. It is the last template of line 4.

Sorry for the details. This is a building project, you know! These templates are your blueprints. Cool!

What fingers should I use on these chords?

A good question, Chester.

Often a fingering is obvious, but when there are choices, it is generally up to what chord fingering preceded and/or follows a chord. The final judge is, what is the easiest way for you to play the chord?

The TAB Music Notation Language

Tab (short for "tablature") is used to help in translating a traditionally notated example. Tab is a notation language in which the six guitar strings are represented by six horizontal lines (see figure I.4). The bottom line is the low E string, and the top line is the high E string. The note is represented by a number indicating the fret at which the note is played. A 0 indicates that the string is played open. In figure I.4, the first note is an open G string, indicated by the zero. The next two notes are a C♯ and a D found on the 2nd and 3rd frets of the second string, the B string.

The Standard Music Notation Language

You do not have to be able to read music to understand the construction process and work with this book. Standard music notation is used occasionally during construction along with the easy-to-read chord templates simply to display the architecture of harmonic structures and help in an explanation. In standard music notation, direction and distances between notes are visually consistent and clearly accompany the technical descriptions in the text. Knowing the name and location of notes on the fingerboard is very important. In chapter 1, a guitar fingerboard "puzzle" will challenge you and help you learn these locations.

Here are some standard guitar-related standard notation symbols. I do strongly encourage you to learn to read standard notation. It will open up many musical doors for you. With practice, reading music becomes as easy as reading words. Which, you may forget, also took a lot of practice!

THE "GUITAR" CLEF

The guitar clef is simply a G clef with a cute little number 8 hanging on the bottom like a teeny ornament. It is used in standard notation examples during construction. Here it is in action.

Fig. I.4. The "Guitar Clef in Action"

This clef simply indicates that the notes, when played on the guitar, sound one octave lower than concert pitch—how a piano would sound those same notes. The guitar is a naturally transposing instrument. It sounds down one octave from written concert pitch.

STRING INDICATIONS

In traditional notation, circled numbers indicate the string on which particular notes are to be played. With a pile of notes (a chord), a circled number indicates the string to be used for the top note, thereby acting as a general position marker.

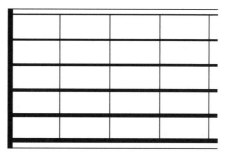

① indicates the high E string
② indicates the B string
③ indicates the G string
④ indicates the D string
⑤ indicates the A string
⑥ indicates the low E string

Fig. I.5. String Indications

O indicates to use an open string for a note.

In text, the term "String Set" refers to a group of strings to be used for a chord.

String Set ① ② ③ indicates that the high E string, B string, and G string are to be used for playing a particular chord form.

FINGER INDICATIONS

In traditional notation, numbers without circles indicate what fingerboard-hand fingers to use for particular notes.

1 indicates the index finger.

2 indicates the middle finger.

3 indicates the ring finger.

4 indicates the pinky.

POSITION INDICATIONS

In standard notation, fingerboard position may be indicated in Roman numerals above the staff to indicate a fret or, as mentioned earlier, with a circled number to indicate the string to be used for a particular top note of a chord. For example, the Roman numeral **III** indicates 3rd position as the fret that a chord or melody note starts on.

Figure I.6 is an example of the guitar notation indications in action with a chord. This is the same chord form used in figure I.1 for the Chord Template Language illustration. This GMaj7(6) chord is in 3rd position (the Roman numeral III). The top note, E natural, is played on the 2nd string or B string (the 2 in the circle), and the fourth finger is used for this note (the uncircled 4). Whew! Sorry about the lingo.

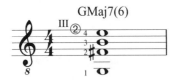

Fig. I.6. GMaj7(6) in Traditional Notation

The Chord Symbol Language

In popular music idioms, from country music to fusion, chord symbols make up an important language. Unfortunately, there is no standard chord-symbol language. The only agreement is that the starting letter of a chord symbol represents the root of the chord. After that, anything goes. In fact, the GMaj7(6) chord symbol used for the previous graphic examples may be seen with these possible alternatives.

GMaj7(6) GM7(6)

GMa7(6) G△7(6)

GMaj($^6_7$) G$\bar{7}$(6)

And those are not all the possibilities! When a new chord quality is introduced, I will make note of possible alternatives you may see.

Here is a general look at some alternatives.

Major may be indicated by **Major** or **Maj** or **Ma** or a triangle (△).

In the case of a major triad, simply using an uppercase letter to indicate the root of the major triad is sufficient: F.

Major 7 may occasionally be written as $\bar{7}$.

Minor may be indicated by **Minor** or **Min** or **min** or with a dash (–).

Flat may be indicated by a flat sign ♭ or a dash (–).

Sharp may be indicated by a sharp sign ♯ or a plus sign + or **Aug**, the abbreviation for augmented.

Diminished may be indicated by **Dim** or **dim** or a small circle (○).

The **Minor 7♭5** chord quality may be indicated by (ø).

A **suspended fourth** may be indicated by **SUSP 4** or **sus4**.

A **slash** / represents the word "over" for triads over bass notes. For example **E/C** represents an E major triad over the bass note C.

A horizontal line —— represents the word "over" for *polychords*: a chord over a chord. For example $\frac{E}{C}$ represents an E major triad over a C major triad.

In my playing experiences, I am still finding many interpretations of chord symbols. You will gradually come across many unique ones yourself.

Harmonic shorthand or use of symbols representing chords and progressions is nothing new. A harmonic shorthand was used back in the 16th century! A chord symbol language called *thoroughbass* or *figured bass* was used in the Baroque period of classical music.

The Interval Language

As we will see, observing chords purely by interval language is a good thing. These "pure intervallic" observations may inspire us to harmonic discoveries or ideas for composing and improvising that may not be as obvious in the chord symbol language. Numbers in boxes indicate an interval or group of intervals.

$\boxed{\flat 7}$ indicates a flat 7th.

$\boxed{46}$ indicates a perfect 4th and a major 6th.

These language details will become second nature to you as construction proceeds.

DELIVERY: MEETING MR. B

> *"It's not how much you've got that's important, it's how well you use what you've got that is."*
>
> —Mr. B., a good friend

I am still trying to learn this lesson from a legendary guitarist of the Boston area. Let's call him "Mr. B" for now. Mr. B. could comp (accompany) with chords beautifully. His awareness of chord vocabulary was impressive, but what Mr. B. could really do was deliver that vocabulary. His groove—sense of rhythm, touch, tone—was magical. He made me realize how the "piles" of information I had accumulated could easily pull my hands to places that my heart could care less about. Much like a recent political speech, perhaps? In our compilation of chord forms during our construction project, let's not forget Mr. B.'s lesson. It is the delivery of the music that makes it work or not.

Throughout our building project, as chord qualities are introduced, I will sketch or make note of musical phrases using the chord quality in action—along with other chords to help us hear and play that chord quality in context.

Seeing words in context helps me understand them. Is it the same with chords, Jon?

It sure is, Chester. In a bit, I will show some direct analogies using chord progressions and sentences.

Earlier, I mentioned the first time I met a major 7th chord. Heavenly! But my first diminished 7th chord experience did not go so smoothly. How could a chord do this to me! As I played a diminished 7th chord the first time, it sounded almost sinister. I backed off, until later, I realized that a diminished 7th chord was an important part in the world of harmonic cadence—as important as the sexier chords. So now, when I meet a new chord, I give it a hug and add it to my creative resources. Some of the stranger harmonic characters I have met have been the most productive!

Let's play the "in action" chord examples throughout the book with Mr. B. in mind.

CADENCE AND MELODIC POWER

Gravity and Magnetism at Work

A dictionary is basically a collection of information, traditionally words. In our chord-dictionary building project, we are collecting chords, one by one. But chords, like words, are part of a lineage. They are used in sentences—in music language, "phrases." These phrases and sentences are simply cadences—motions from REST to ACTION to REST.

REST	ACTION	REST
"I	love	pizza."

Above, "I love pizza" is an example of a cadence using words. When we put chords together in a progression, they make a musical cadence, going between points of rest and action.

When I present harmonic cadences here, I use standard notation and chord templates to show how tones move upward or downward between chords. Melodic motions upward create magnetic effect, and melodic motions downward create gravitational effect, keeping those chords resolving and working!

In chord symbol language, a simple example of this cadence is illustrated here in chord templates and then in standard notation. Play and listen to the cadence.

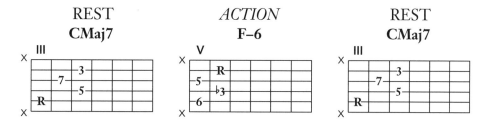

Fig. I.7. CMaj7 to F–6 to CMaj7

Now, here with the above chords illustrated in traditional notation, the motion of the chord notes of the CMaj7 chord moving up to the notes of F–6, creating tension, then returning gravitationally back to rest, CMaj7 is seen clearly.

Fig. I.8. CMaj7 to F–6 to CMaj7

Chords would be out of a job if it weren't for the power of melodic motion. Please enjoy playing and delivering the harmonic phrases I offer throughout our project. Feel the cadences—the personalities of the chords.

I get how those chords move now, thanks!

Speaking of personalities, I am reading a fascinating book, *The Professor and the Madman*, by Simon Winchester. The book is subtitled "A Tale of Murder, Insanity, and the Making of the *Oxford English Dictionary*." As dry as the subtitle sounds, so far the book has been pretty cool. I am about halfway through the book at this point and will keep you posted. I hope our dictionary project doesn't get quite that dramatic. Strange enough, about forty years ago when I first started on my first chord explorations, as a much newer guitarist, someone mentioned to me, "I heard about a guy who tried to learn every guitar chord known to peoplekind and eventually lost his mind!" It is probably that phrase that kindled my tireless infinite search for new chords, and I now realize the search is not unlike the search for the Holy Grail.

Most importantly, I hope the construction process not only increases your awareness of chord structures technically but also inspires and becomes a creative catalyst for your compositional and improvisational explorations. Good luck!

M O N A D S : 1 - P A R T C H O R D S

SOME COOL TECHNICALITIES

At first, I began constructing my chord dictionary with intervals or dyads: 2-part chords, since they are such an important element in the building and understanding process of chords. I then realized, and thanks to Mother Nature, that there are even simpler chords, which I call *monads*: 1-note chords. At first, I thought I had coined a new word, but as the *American Heritage Dictionary* (Third Edition. Houghton-Mifflin, 1992) says:

> **Mo-nad** n. 1. Philos. An indivisible impenetrable unit of substance viewed as the basic constituent element of physical reality in the metaphysics of Liebnitz. 2. Biol. A single-celled microorganism, esp. a flaggelate protozoan of the genus Monas. 3. Chem. An atom or a radical with valence 1.

Since there was no music connotation in the *American Heritage Dictionary*, I also tried the *Harvard Dictionary of Music*, and "monad" was nowhere to be found. Next, I will try the honcho (Japanese for "boss") of all music dictionaries, *The Groves Dictionary of Music*, and let you know if "monad" is listed.

Can you check that out for me, Chester?

Sure, Jon!

When a monad, or a single "fundamental" note sounds, other notes also softly sound, sympathetically creating a subtle chord. These additional notes are called *harmonics*, *overtones*, or *partials*. They strongly affect the sound quality of the fundamental note, and also how it "gets along" or harmonizes with other fundamental notes. An easy way to observe harmonics is by playing a low note on the piano with the sustain pedal pressed down. You will hear the fundamental's overtones inspiring the other strings to ring.

Let's play and listen carefully to a monad on the guitar. Play your low open E string, and listen carefully for any other notes. Strike the string a bit harder or nearer to the bridge, if needed. As you focus in, you will eventually hear a subtle chord that consists of the obvious open E note along with other overtones. The most prominent note is another E note, an octave higher, and then a higher B note and a G# note, quite soft. These overtones create a subtle, very soft E major triad—an essential chord quality we will meet a bit later, on the third floor. With practice, you will also start to hear a D note, which suggests a dominant 7th chord. We'll also meet that chord quality a bit later.

I actually hear the G# note louder than the other notes.

Where you strike the strings will incite some harmonics more than others, Chester.

This is subtle stuff, but these powerful elements are constantly at play, as we explore and build our dictionary. *Horns, Strings, and Harmony* by Arthur H. Benade (Dover Publications, 1992) is a wonderful book that looks into the fantastic world of acoustics, of which harmonics are a most important part.

For chord explorers, it is important to know where all the monads are on the guitar. With this ability, many techniques for creative guitar playing will open up to you.

Here is a partially started template of the guitar fingerboard. Observe the patterns and complete the rest of the fingerboard as a reference guide. Work in pencil. If you need a hint, a complete fingerboard template is in the "Tool Box" chapter (figure 14.3), which you can photocopy for easy reference. It will come in handy during our construction process.

THE FINGERBOARD PUZZLE

I started it, now you finish it. Check the completed fingerboard template in the "Tool Box" chapter for the solution.

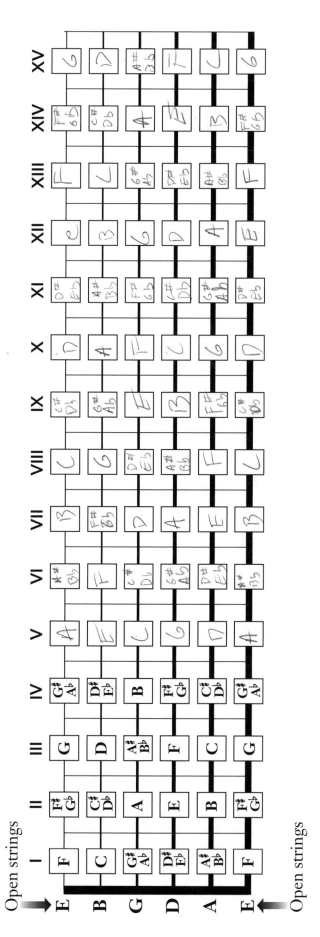

Fig. 1.1. Fingerboard Puzzle

Now, up to the second-floor chapter, "Dyads: 2-Part Chords," where we can check out how monads get along—or do *not* get along—with each other, and where they are on the guitar.

CHAPTER 2: SECOND FLOOR

DYADS: 2-PART CHORDS

INTERVALS: THE SYLLABLES OF CHORDS

OUR GROUNDBREAKING CEREMONY!

Oh by the way, Jon, "monad" wasn't in Groves Dictionary of Music!

Already we're breaking new ground, Chester—our own original music-language word!

Just as the words of a language dictionary are composed of syllables—the basic building blocks of words—our chord dictionary should include intervals, the basic building blocks of chords. An interval is the pitch distance between two notes. Each interval has its own distinct sound and quality that defines the sound quality and naming of a chord. These intervals, or dyads (2-part chords), are very complete sounds in themselves. Remember our look at the surprisingly rich world of monads, the 1-note chords? Imagine two monads sounding simultaneously and each of their cool overtones interacting, creating very distinct chemistries or qualities.

In fact, two notes sounding together is a lot of music. Listen to Johann Sebastian Bach's two-part inventions, the vocalizations of Simon and Garfunkel, the guitar inventions of Jim Hall and Jimmy Raney, and Yikes! Béla Bartók's violin duets are pretty complete listening experiences, if you ask me! In fact, many sections of compositions for full orchestra consist of only two parts, each part doubled (repeated) at the unison (same notes) or octave through the instruments. The various instrument tone colors further enrich the sound. Intervals, or 2-part chords, are important foundations for 2-part counterpoint technique on the guitar and also make for wonderful textural contrasts to single-note melodic ideas and the triads (3-part chords) and the 4-, 5-, and 6-part chords we will explore during construction. In fact, the larger chord forms and qualities each have a "heartbeat" called guide tones that is the essence of the chord, and these guide tones consist of a simple 2-note interval. We will explore guide tones a bit later in this chapter, and in later chapters as well.

PURE INTERVALLIC OBSERVATION BY SIGHT AND SOUND

It is important to be able to see, observe, and describe chords purely by interval. Chord symbol language has its place for communicating a musical idea, but "pure intervallic" observations will give you an architectural view that may inspire ideas for composing and improvising that may not be as obvious in the chord symbol language.

It is also very important to be able to hear, observe, and describe chords purely by interval. As we build our Intervals/Dyads Templates, play them and create your own sound association with each interval. This will help you remember the interval not only as a visual shape but also as a sound "personality" or quality.

These initial perceptions may change depending on the context in which an interval is heard. As each interval is introduced for the building process, I will give general music language descriptions of that interval's basic quality and examples of the interval in action that you can play and hear for yourself.

At the end of this chapter, I will share an ear study to help interval recognition and a *Million Dollar Idea* with you.

Count me in, Jon!

Stay tuned!

Since this is a chord dictionary—a harmonic thesis, if you will—the two notes of these intervals will be played simultaneously on two different strings, producing harmony, which we can define as "the simultaneous combination and sounding of multiple notes." Intervals are also important building blocks for single-note studies.

START GROUNDBREAKING!

Grab a blank template (see figure 14.1 of the "Tools" chapter). Don't forget to sharpen that pencil, write clearly, and keep your templates in your Dictionary Binder. A 2-inch thick binder should do. We can now officially start our groundbreaking ceremony.

If a chord fingering is difficult, try moving it up the fingerboard for study, as the distances shorten between frets.

Some intervals/dyads will have more fingering possibilities than others. Use the Whole Fingerboard Template you completed in chapter 1 for reference, if needed. No open strings, please. A later stage of construction will cover those possibilities.

As with the rest of our building project, I will set your template into motion. It is up to you to complete it as well as you can. Label this first template, at the top, "Intervals/Dyads: Page 1."

THE UNISON

As an important foundation for building the rest of the intervals, let's officially break ground with the simplest and smallest interval, and the most difficult to play: the unison. A unison is formed by playing two of the same note at the same time.

So there is no sound distance between the two notes of that interval, Jon!?

Yes, Chester, and as you will quickly notice, unison doesn't coincide with easy-to-grab!

The shortest distance between two notes is a unison? It sounds easy.

It sounds simple, but playing unisons on the guitar, without open strings, is difficult because of the stretch involved. Let's start with the friendliest unison fingering, besides using an open string, to help us out. Play a C note on the 1st fret of our B string along with the C note on the 5th fret of our G string. Here is the unison displayed in traditional and tablature notation as well as on a chord template. A unison's basic quality is described as an "open consonance"—pretty mild-sounding stuff (when in tune, of course…).

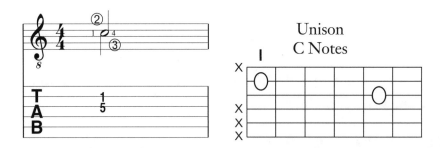

Fig. 2.1. Unison C Notes

Now, let's find fingering forms for unisons elsewhere on the fingerboard, on the other possible two string sets. To get us started, I have fully illustrated the unison interval possibilities in figure 2.2. Copy them and label each one "unison" on your template.

Notice that there are five fingering possibilities for a unison: the fingering form in figure 2.1 found on the G and B strings (which are a major third apart) and the four other form possibilities found on the other adjacent two string sets (which are a perfect fourth apart). That is a total of five fingering possibilities for the unison (see figure 2.2).

Please note that these templates have the infinity symbol (∞) for the fret. These fingerings can be played anywhere along the string set. In fact, playing these stretchy unisons further up the fingerboard is a lot easier. Have faith! The rest of the intervals are easier to grab. Actually, I enjoy using the unison in soloing. The doubling of a note has a nice fat sound.

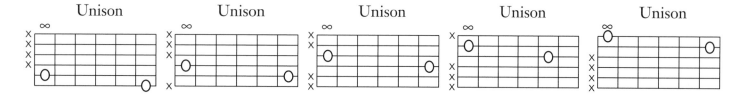

Fig. 2.2. Unisons on All String Sets

Hold it a second, Jon. What is this major third apart and perfect fourth stuff?

I'm sorry, Chester, I was getting ahead of myself.

THE INTERVALS CHART

A "major third" and a "perfect fourth" are other types of intervals. To clarify, let me illustrate the intervals we will be building from the note C, shown in traditional notation, where it's easiest to see them.

1. The first interval is the unison. It is simply the same pitch or note played with itself! Let's call it "one" for now.

2. The next interval is the second. On a music staff, a second is from a note on a line to an adjacent space or from a space to an adjacent line, depending on where you start.

3. A third is from either a space to a next space or from a line to a next line.

You can also easily tabulate an interval on a music staff by counting the lines and spaces used by the two notes of an interval.

This pattern continues as the intervals become larger. Prefixes, such as major or minor, natural or flat, perfect or sharp, and diminished or augmented, indicate a half-step difference in size between intervals. For example, a minor second and a major second are a half step apart. Also, as you can see, some intervals can have several different names such as augmented 4th and sharp 4th.

THE INTERVALS CHART

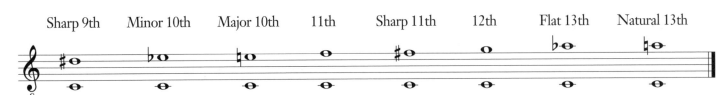

Fig. 2.3. The Intervals Chart

I need to have a guitar-fingerboard view of what intervals are all about, Jon.

Okay Chester, let's take a look at a monochord for a moment.

A mono-who?!?!

ANOTHER LOOK AT INTERVALS: THE MONOCHORD

A zither-like single string instrument, called a monochord, has been used since ancient times to study musical phenomena. Let's grab one for a second to take a fingerboard-view of intervals at play.

Where do we find a monochord, Jon?

Actually, Chester, holding our guitar is like having six monochords at one time!

We'll use just one of our guitar's strings for interval illustration, for now. Here in figure 2.4 is just the B string, our guitar's second string. We will use the 1st fret C note as a reference point to see the intervals.

Let's call the C note the first interval (unison). If we move a fret distance higher up the string to D♭ (C♯), we have moved an interval distance of a minor second: C to D♭ (C♯).

Another fret movement higher now creates a major second: C to D. Another fret movement creates a minor third: C to E♭ (D♯), then major third, and so forth. See figure 2.4 for the rest of the interval names. I have illustrated the intervals up to an octave.

For our chord explorations, we will be playing the two notes of these intervals at the same time, using two strings simultaneously. This creates *harmonic* intervals. The one-string, monochord-like example illustrates the simplest way to view interval distance on the guitar: along one string, as *melodic* intervals. The challenge here comes in learning to see and play these intervals simultaneously as harmonic intervals: from string to string.

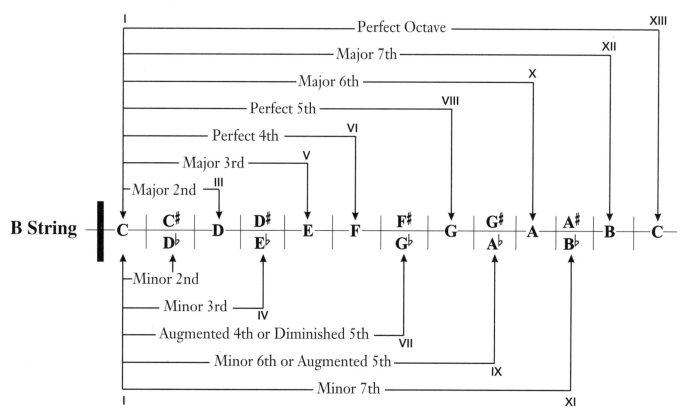

Fig. 2.4. The Monochord

I may again "get ahead of myself" and use in a "musical context" example some intervals that will be introduced later in the construction process. For now, just play the example. There is no better way to meet an interval or chord than by playing and hearing it in action.

For the rest of the intervals, I will give only the first form or fingering of each one. You find the rest. I will let you know how many forms I found, just to guide your explorations. Keep your full Fingerboard Template you completed from chapter 1 handy as a reference.

THE MINOR SECOND

Now for a real interval! Take the unison, and stretch one of the notes one fret—a half step—to create a minor second.

Stretch!! You gotta be kidding me, Jon! That unison was tough enough.

I know, Chester.

Actually, as you will see, the minor second will be physically easier to play than the unison. At least, one fret distance easier.

This interval will sound intense since there are some serious vibrations at play! Especially, this first fingering on the bottom string set. Remember to try the fingering higher up along the strings to ease the stretch. Here is the unison form moving to a minor second form on the bottom two strings.

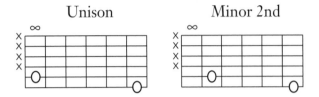

Fig. 2.5. Unison to Minor Second

Using the unison shapes (figure 2.2) we just sketched in on our Intervals/Dyads Template as a guide, stretch the unison forms a fret and sketch in the minor-second possibilities from them. You should find five possibilities. Don't forget to label each one "minor second."

On the guitar fingerboard, distances can sure be deceiving!

Right, Chester. In fact, in the above template examples, the notes of the unison to the minor second are visually moving closer together, even though the minor second is a larger interval or distance than the unison (one)!

Remember to let the interval sounds inspire you. Find a "mnemonic"—a memory aid—to use as a relationship that helps you remember the interval sound.

In a concert performance with the Boston Pops Orchestra and John Williams, we played the soundtrack from Alfred Hitchcock's film *Psycho*. In the shower scene section from the film, the violins were pumping some serious minor seconds! Unforgettable. Scary!

The minor second can also sound quite beautiful.

Of course, beauty is in the ear of the beholder.

Wonderfully said, Chester.

The general music language description of a minor second's basic quality is sharp dissonance, or pretty rich stuff. In another context, or when heard as part of a larger structure, this same interval may sound different.

Here in the next playing example are some minor seconds in action, as integral parts of chords. Play the chords and give a listen. Your earlobes may curl up! Me, I think it's purty. Try different deliveries. Refer to the template language section in the Introduction, if needed. Don't forget the open strings, to be used for the roots of each chord. And don't forget that Roman numerals indicate particular frets for chord positions on the fingerboard. Notice the minor second between the minor 3rd degree (♭3) and the 9th degree (9) of the A–(9) chord and the minor second between the root and the flat-9th degree of the E7(♭9) chord. That stretch will give those minor seconds away! The details of these chord qualities will be discussed later in construction. Right now, play them, meet them, and enjoy their personalities.

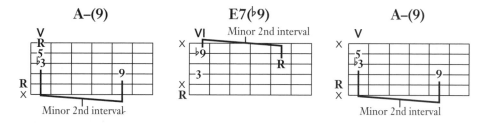

Fig. 2.6. A–(9) and E7(♭9). The Minor Second at Work.

Having that guitar tuned well is really important here!

As a very important part of our delivery, having our instrument well tuned will make or break a musical statement, Chester.

THE MAJOR SECOND

Stretch those minor seconds we just sketched in on our Dyads Template Sheet one fret. The minor second becomes a major second. This quality is considered a mild dissonance. Find five possibilities. In figure 2.7, the minor second form moves to a major second on the bottom two strings.

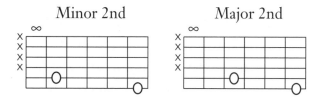

Fig. 2.7. Minor Second Moving to Major Second

Here is a form for a C major triad with an added 2nd degree, C(2), moving to a C/F chord (a slash chord). Notice the major second in each of these chords. For me, the major second adds a nice richness to these chords. Repeat it as a vamp. Sweet.

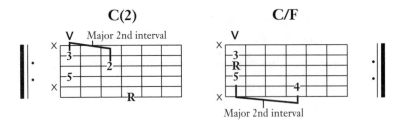

Fig. 2.8. C(2) to C/F Vamp

 I'm ready for a break, Jon. This interval stuff is tough on the hands!

Good idea, Chester. Check out the yoga hand stretches in the Break Room, chapter 12.

Thanks, Jon!

THE MINOR THIRD

Now, grab your hard hat, take those major seconds, and stretch the top note up a notch (a fret) to make them minor thirds. Notice how the intervals are becoming easier to play. The humble minor third, as we will see in the "Third Floor, Triads" chapter, is an integral part of the major triad as well as the minor and diminished triads. The minor third is referred to as a soft consonance. Here is the major second form moving to a minor third form on the bottom two strings.

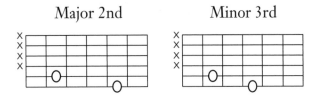

Fig. 2.9. Major Second to Minor Third

I found five possibilities for the minor third.

As mentioned earlier, chords would be out of a job if it weren't for the power of melodic motion. For a very simple example of this, play a major second, then move the lower note to create a minor third. A simple "Amen" cadence or resolution occurs. Not earth-shattering, but these simple, powerful motions not only keep chords working but us guitarists too! These forces are at play even in the larger glitzier chords. Without this underlying power, they would be just more pretty faces. Here is this simple cadence motion in standard notation and in chord template.

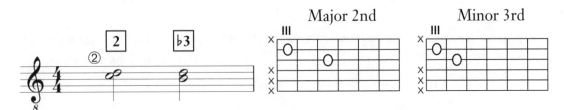

Fig. 2.10. A-men

Say Jon, those yoga stretches felt really good!

And they are good for your hand and arm health, Chester. Let's build some major third templates.

THE MAJOR THIRD

Let's brighten up those minor thirds a bit and make them major thirds, just a one-fret stretch. The major third is also an integral part of the major and minor triads, as we shall see on the third floor (chapter 3). The major third is also considered a soft consonance. As with the last several intervals, I found five possibilities for the major third on the adjacent string sets. Here is the first one.

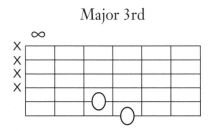

Fig. 2.11. Major Third

When I play these minor and major thirds on the higher strings, I am reminded of those romantic serenades. In fact, Romeo may have been using these guys in his serenade to Juliet, probably on his mandolin.

As wacky as they may seem, personal reactions like these really help me connect with a sound and remember it.

You fooled me, Jon. You're one of those romantic types....

I guess so, Chester.

THE PERFECT FOURTH

The perfect fourth is considered a dual personality, quality-wise. In musical situations, this interval may sound consonant when surrounded by dissonant neighbors or dissonant when surrounded by consonant neighbors. In fact, this flexibility makes fourths popular for building harmonies. Music from Palestrina to Chick Corea is testament to this. To create the perfect fourth, move the major third's top note up a fret. As you play a major third moving to a perfect fourth, notice how the perfect fourth likes to return to the major third. It's that "Amen" thing again, from another angle. I could find five possibilities for the perfect fourth. Here's the first one.

Perfect 4th

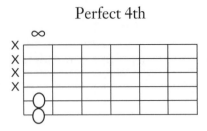

Fig. 2.12. Perfect Fourth

Here is an example of simple interval cadences. Seconds and fourths are resolving into thirds. Simple, but effective.

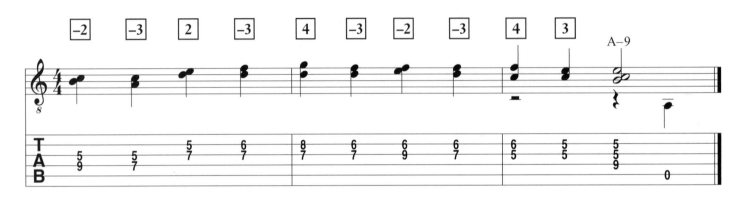

Fig. 2.13. Seconds and Fourths Resolving into Thirds

The perfect fourth can also stand on its own very well. Here are some 3-note chords (triads) built primarily in perfect fourths moving in an E minor scale. Try this example with a low open-E string as accompaniment. Create your own groove, from slow to funky. We will take a close look at various triad possibilities with the Palette Chart when we get up to the "Roof"(chapter 9) of the *Chord Factory*.

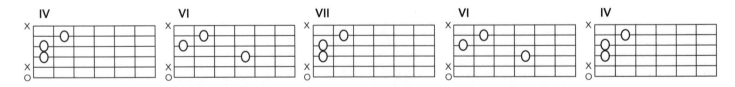

Fig. 2.14. Triads with Perfect Fourths in Action

Sounds like Gregorian Chant!

That is a great association to make for future recognition of the fourth, Chester. Each person will have his or her own personal reaction. Especially when using different deliveries.

At the beginning of this chapter, I mentioned the "heartbeat" or guide tones of chords. The perfect fourth is an essential interval that makes up this heartbeat, as well as the next interval coming right up. I will show some examples of guide tones in action right after we explore the next two intervals: the augmented fourth and the perfect fifth.

THE AUGMENTED FOURTH (SHARP 4) OR DIMINISHED FIFTH
(FORMERLY KNOWN AS THE "DIABOLUS IN MUSICA!")

This interval is also called a *tritone*—a distance of three whole steps or six frets along a string.

Augmented means that an interval has been sharpened a half step (one fret distance); this interval may also be called a diminished fifth. It is the perfect fourth sharpened a bit. This interval, like the perfect fourth, is also considered a dual personality. In musical situations, this interval may sound restful or active. As we will explore a bit later, tritones are the guide tones of dominant 7th chords, and in a blues, they can sound quite restful. On the other hand, in many cadences, the tritone of a dominant 7th chord really demands to be resolved—to come to rest.

As the intervals become larger, more forms become physically possible. I found nine forms for the augmented fourth, since another string set becomes physically possible. I present all nine here for the augmented fourth (tritone) to help you see the possibilities. Refer to the full Fingerboard Template for reference.

Here are the possibilities. Label each of these nine forms ♯4 (augmented fourth) and °5 (diminished fifth).

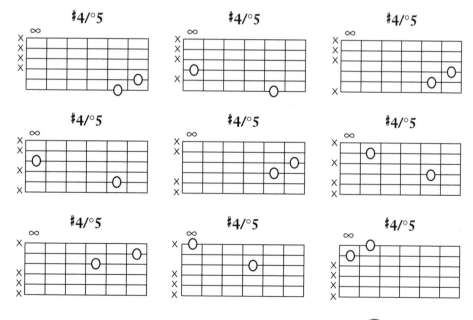

Fig. 2.15. The Nine Possibilities for the ♯4/°5

That finishes up the first page of dyads, Jon.

Good, Chester.

As you will see, the tritone is really a powerful interval. The combination of chromatic motion moving upward (magnetism) and chromatic motion downward (gravity) as it resolves gives it this power, which is one of the most important motions in the harmony business.

Figure 2.16 presents a standard notation and template example for illustration. As we will see in chapter 6, as big as those dominant 7th chords can get with all those fancy tensions on them, without a tritone as their powerful "heartbeat," these chords would be up shi....

Watch it, Jon!!!

Oops.... They would be out of a gig!

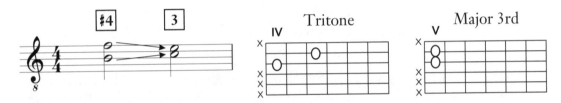

Fig. 2.16. Tritone Resolving to Major Third

Hot diggity, I found gold, Chester!

Whatcha got, Jon?!

As I was exploring the augmented fourth form possibilities, a brand new chord form appeared to me. It is a really cool dominant 7(♯9) chord form I never thought of before. Here it is. It is a nice alternative to the tired Jimi Hendrix sharp 9th chord I always seem to use. Be sure to play the open strings for the roots (R), as indicated. Here it is in action, resolving to a pretty AMaj7(6,9) voicing.

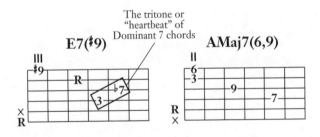

Fig. 2.17. New Dominant 7(♯9)

In chapter 6, we will use Guide Tones Templates to help us find some nice chord voicings.

The cats in the late Middle Ages referred to the augmented fourth as the *diabolus in musica*—the devil in music, or devil's chord. They were tough on everybody back then! I personally really like the augmented fourth, not only as a harmonic sound but also as a melodic sound. Leonard Bernstein agrees and the beautiful opening notes of "Maria" from the musical *West Side Story* is testament to this. And...

Ma-Ri-A...!

Nice singing, Chester!

And the *Simpsons* theme!

And wolves! AH-OOO-OOOOO!!!

Nice, Chester. By the way, the augmented fourth also divides the octave in half! I thought you'd be excited about that.

And the reason we double-labeled the augmented fourth also as a diminished fifth is because when we invert a ♯4, a °5 is the result. They are exactly the same interval distance apart: a tritone. The augmented fourth is the only interval distance and quality that stays the same when inverted. More exciting news!

What do you mean by "inverted," Jon?

Good question. In fact, we should talk a bit about inversions, since this next series of intervals are simply the intervals we just built but upside down!

INVERSION RAP

"Class, today we are going to work on inversions."

—Laura, my very cool yoga teacher

What Laura meant by inversions was yoga positions like the headstand, shoulder stand, and other upside-down-isms. In music harmony language, inversions of intervals work basically the same. What was on the bottom (the feetsies) goes to the top and the top (the head) goes to the bottom. So let's see, and hear, how our dyads take to a little yoga workout.

As Laura would say at the end of each yoga session, "Thank you for your flexibility."

The concept of inversions was an epoch-making discovery of Johannes Lippius, a composer back in the 17th century. Hey, don't take for granted the harmonic liberties we have today. Use the perspective that possibilities for discovery are endless.

Here is a major third. By taking its feetsies (the bottom C note) up an octave and placing it above the E, we now have its inversion: a minor sixth.

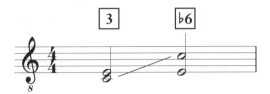

Fig. 2.19. Major Third Inverting to a Minor Sixth

To find the inversion of any interval quickly, subtract that interval from 9. Using the above major third as an example, subtract it from 9 and you have 6, a minor sixth. As you notice, the quality of the interval changes also.

So, when pǝʇɹǝʌuᴉ:

- Major intervals become minor. A major third becomes a minor sixth.
- Minor intervals become major. A minor third becomes a major sixth.
- Perfect intervals stay perfect. A perfect fifth becomes a perfect fourth.
- Augmented intervals become diminished. An augmented fourth becomes a diminished fifth.
- Diminished intervals become augmented. A diminished fifth becomes an augmented fourth.

As we shall see, these inversions may have different characteristics from the original interval. "Complementary interval" is a term used to denote the inversion of an interval. An augmented fourth is the complementary interval of a diminished fifth.

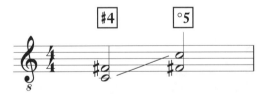

Fig. 2.20. Augmented Fourth Inverting to Diminished Fifth

THE PERFECT FIFTH

You will need a fresh template sheet to continue with the next interval, the perfect fifth. Label this sheet at the top "Dyads/Intervals Page 2."

Stretching an augmented fourth up one fret will produce a solid sounding perfect fifth, which by the way, inverted is a _____. (You fill in the answer.)

You may notice when you sketch the nine possibilities for perfect fifths on your template, that on the bottom strings, a good old rock 'n' roll power chord appears.

This is a testament to the perfect fifth's solid personality. From "Johnny B. Goode," to the Beatles, to Metallica, the fifth is a tried and true sound, an idiomatic foundation! Impressive.

Perfect 5th

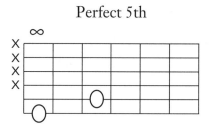

Fig. 2.21. Perfect Fifth

The perfect fifth is also the backbone of triadic harmony—the root and perfect fifth of major and minor triads. The perfect fifth is also a strong overtone. Hopefully, you heard it back in chapter 1 when we explored monads. The music language cats call the perfect fifth an *open consonance*, a mild sound. They just might change their minds if they heard that power chord in action!

For fun, here is a cool sounding chord: a pile of perfect fifths. To me, they sound majestic and solemn. The perfect fifth was also pretty popular back in the days of Gregorian chant.

And they are the inversions of perfect fourths! Relatives!

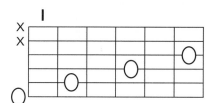

Fig. 2.22. A Flurry of Perfect Fifths

As mentioned earlier, the perfect fifth (along with its relatives, the perfect fourth and augmented fourth) is also an integral part of the linear motion of chord progressions, serving as guide tones of some chord qualities.

What exactly are these guide tones all about, Jon?

Here is a look at guide tones, Chester.

THE GUIDE TONES OR "HEARTBEATS" OF CHORDS

Each chord quality has its own distinctive guide tones consisting of the 3rd and 7th degrees of the chord, creating a 2-note interval. The guide tones of a major 7th chord creates a perfect fifth between its 3rd and 7th degrees, inverted a perfect fourth. The guide tones of a minor 7th chord also creates a perfect fifth, and as we have seen, the augmented fourth or diminished fifth makes up the 3rd and 7th of the dominant 7th chord.

These "2-note chords," the guide tones, create powerful linear motion through a chord progression. Here are the opening eight bars of a classic standard tune "Autumn Leaves," stated using only the guide tones—the 3rd and 7th degrees of each chord quality. No roots or any cool sounding tensions. Just the guide tones.

AUTUMN LEAVES GUIDE TONES

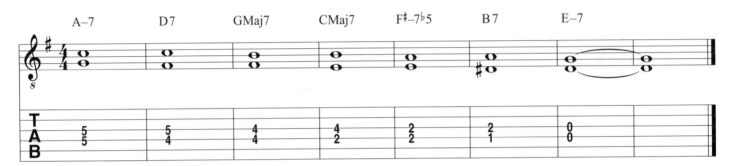

Fig. 2.23. "Autumn Leaves" Guide Tones

These guide tones are pretty powerful!

Yes they are, Chester. They keep those chords working for us.

Later, when we explore the addition of two or more tensions (chapter 6), we will use the basic guide tones as a visual foundation with some Guide Tone Templates to help us squeeze some more voicing possibilities from that fingerboard.

Say Jon, how can I learn the spellings for all these intervals?

Back in the "Tool Box" chapter is the Interval Cross-Reference Chart. It works like a mileage chart. Check it out, Chester. You can also use it to help you with the Chord Symbols CrossTones Puzzle in the "Break" chapter.

THE MINOR SIXTH/AUGMENTED FIFTH

Depending on context, this interval may be called a minor sixth (♭6) or an augmented fifth (♯5). Both will come into the construction process in the "Fourth Floor, 4-Part Chords" chapter. The minor sixth, being an inversion of a _____, is considered a soft consonance.

I found nine possibilities by stretching those perfect fifths a bit by one fret. What comes to mind when you play this interval color? Remember to try it in different contexts. Play it sweet, crank it next to a power chord, or be mellow. In fact, maybe Romeo was using these interval guys, higher up the fretboard, to impress Juliet. Along with the major sixth, coming up next.

Minor 6th

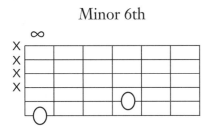

Fig. 2.24. Minor Sixth

THE MAJOR SIXTH/DIMINISHED SEVENTH

Pull those minor sixths up a fret to create the major sixth, also considered a soft consonance. I found nine possibilities. I was playing these major sixth forms sliding along the higher strings along with the minor sixth forms, and they reminded me of a funny Luau scene from an episode of *Love Boat*.

Major 6th

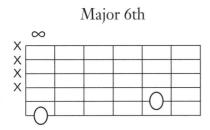

Fig. 2.25. Major Sixth

Here, I am harmonizing the ending of a simple lullaby, composed for my children, with a sequence of sixths and thirds with an occasional fifth for contrast. Try taking a simple melody, and try it yourself. I am using an open D string for support.

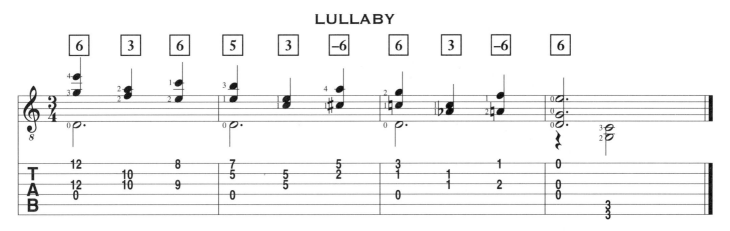

Fig. 2.26. Lullaby

The possibilities are endless. Here is one of my favorite quotes, by Vincent Persechetti, an inspiring composer.

"Intervals can follow each other in any order and may be arranged to form any pattern of tension interplay."

Wow! I like that attitude.

I do, too, Chester.

THE MINOR SEVENTH (♭7)

The minor seventh, also called flat seven, being the inversion of the _____, is considered a mild dissonance. It has a bit of a buzz and an active tendency to come back to rest to a sixth, of which it is a close neighbor. Here is a minor seventh.

Minor 7th

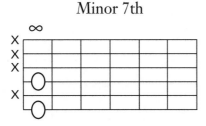

Fig. 2.27. Minor Seventh

I found six possibilities for the minor seventh. It is a nice interval to use melodically, and again, Leonard Bernstein agrees. The minor seventh is used beautifully to begin his tune "Somewhere," also from *West Side Story*. Some folks call this tune "There's a Place for Us."

There's... a... place... for us...!

Perfect, Chester! You sang that beautifully. You oughta be in pictures.

I just love that show.

It certainly sounds like you do.

Tony and Maria, the characters in *West Side Story*, sing it beautifully. Check it out.

As you can hear again, using opening bits of common tunes to trigger an interval sound works well. Find your own.

Remember that all this interval construction work will also certainly inspire your melodic ideas as composers and improvisers.

THE MAJOR SEVENTH

Bringing the minor seventh up a bit to major seventh creates a powerful interval—a *sharp dissonance*, in textbook lingo. It has a strong tendency to move down to a sixth, move up to an octave, or just stay put. Remember that any interval or chord can go to any other interval or chord at any time. It's up to you. Just like words. There are lots of choices, but not all of them make sense. It is up to you to do the communicating!

I found six fingering possibilities for this rich puppy. Here is one of them.

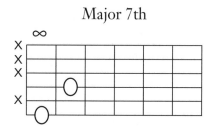

Fig. 2.28. Major Seventh

Here is a simple study using sevenths and sixths. I am simply moving from the richer sounding sevenths to the more restful sixths, creating simple cadences using a Lydian major mode or scale. It is simply "pure intervallic" thinking. Try your own combinations of intervals. There are lots to find.

And don't forget "Mr. B's" lesson. Delivery!

SEVENTHS TO SIXTHS STUDY

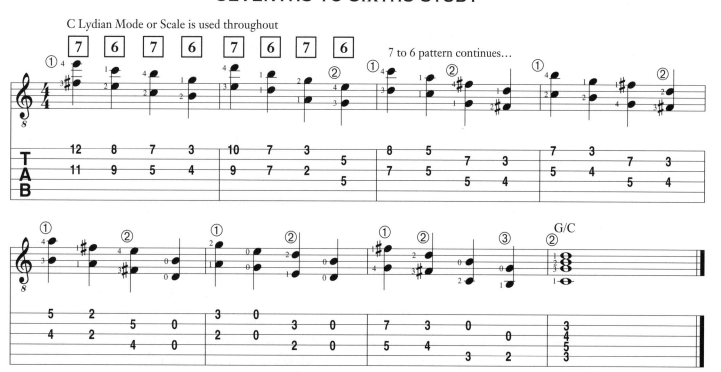

Fig. 2.29. Sevenths to Sixths Study

I like playing this as a schmaltzy waltz!

Nice approach, Chester. These ideas are here to be explored. Try your own possibilities also.

THE OCTAVE

When we stretch that major seventh up one fret, an octave is created. The octave is considered a perfect consonance and rightly so (like the unison, when it's in tune!). It is also powerful. Just for now, let's think of the octave as an "eighth," to help with our transition to the compound intervals coming up. I found seven possibilities for the octave. Here is my first. I also needed to start a fresh template sheet, Dyads/Intervals Page 3, to help with the compound intervals.

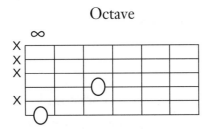

Fig. 2.30. Octave

The octave has power. It is the first overtone of a note and is a common simple harmonization for melodic lines. The great guitar playing of Wes Montgomery provides many wonderful examples. Consider the power of a simple melody when "harmonized" with octaves through the instruments of a full orchestra!

The octave is also the threshold for the compound intervals, which are simply all the intervals we just built, but now with an octave added.

Some...where...o...ver...the...rainbow!...

You sang that octave a little out-of-tune there, Chester! But another good tune reference for an interval.

First, I need a break. I'm going to continue reading Simon Winchester's *The Professor and the Madman*, the book I mentioned earlier. WOW! William Minor, the main character from Simon Winchester's dictionary book, was a heavy cat! He was a major contributor to the first *Oxford English Dictionary*, and he did it all from his maximum-security cell in an asylum in Britain! I will keep you posted, but first let's check out the compound intervals for our own dictionary.

THE COMPOUND INTERVALS

Intervals larger than an octave (an eighth) are called *compound intervals*. (Those smaller intervals we just finished are called *simple intervals*.) Adding an octave strengthens the fourths and fifths, makes the thirds and sixths more resonant, and brightens the sound of the richer intervals: seconds and sevenths. Compound intervals will also be found as extensions and will be explored a bit later (chapter 5, "5-Part Chords"). To find the compound interval of a simple interval, add 7 to the simple interval. A simple interval of a fifth is a compound interval of a twelfth.

THE MINOR NINTH OR FLAT 9 (♭9)

If that augmented fourth—that diabolus in musica—made those 17th century cats nervous, I can't imagine what a minor ninth would do. They'd probably cut its head off and make it a nice polite octave; it is larger than an octave by a minor second. I found five possibilities for this sharp dissonance.

Minor 9th

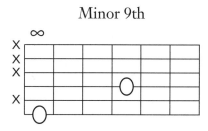

Fig. 2.31. Minor Ninth

Today, jazz cats can't seem to get enough of the ♭9. They dish it up in dominant 7(♭9) chords and in interestingly voiced major 7 and minor chords. Here is an interesting open-string form I found recently for a C–(9) chord. A ♭9 is found between the chord's 9th degree (the open D string) and the minor 3rd degree. In figure 2.32, the flat ninths are boxed in for detail. The flat ninth makes the chord sound dark and interesting. Here is the form along with another new form I found for a G7(♭9) chord, also with a flat ninth between the low root and the flat 9th degree. It has no 3rd degree. Thanks to the open strings on these forms! We will further explore the amazing world of open-string possibilities in "Open Strings," chapter 8.

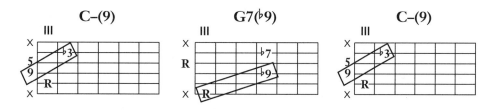

Fig. 2.32. Cool Voicings with Flat Ninths

THE MAJOR NINTH

For the major ninth (or natural ninth), there are again five form possibilities! Watch the stretches. Common sense. Don't injure yourself.

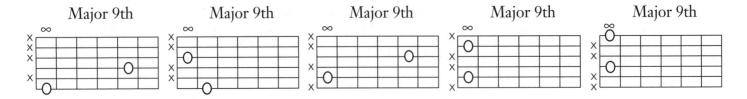

Fig. 2.33. The Five Major-Ninth Interval Possibilities

Notice how in figure 2.34, the natural ninth has a nice bright quality on the A major triad, with the added 9 voicing moving to the D7(9) voicing. The ninth is found between the root and natural 9th degrees of both these chords. Hang out with this vamp for a bit. It's cool.

The French Impressionist composer Claude Debussy loved 9th chords! Voila!!!

And James Brown, the Godfather.

I feel good!!! Na na na na na na na!

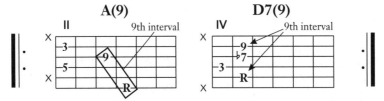

Fig. 2.34. A(9) to D7(9) Vamp

THE SHARP NINTH (♯9)/MINOR TENTH (♭10)

As the sharp ninth's name indicates, raise or sharpen the major ninth a fret. With the sharp ninth, there are three possible forms. Here is the first.

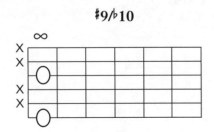

Fig. 2.35. Sharp Ninth

As with all structures, context is important. This interval can possibly appear mildly as part of an open minor triad, called a minor tenth in this case, or as an intense part of a cool dominant 7(♯9) chord between the root and sharp 9th degree à la Hendrix. Notice again how these larger intervals brighten things up. Here is an A–(9) and an E7(♯9) voicing to show the natural ninth and sharp ninths in action. The ninths are found between the root and 9th degrees. Don't forget the open strings for the A–(9) chord.

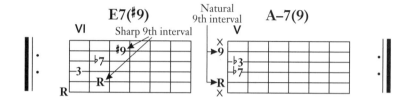

Fig. 2.36. E7(♯9) and A–(9) Vamp

I found a nice sharp spicy major 7th in that last E7(♯9) chord, Jon.

Right, Chester—between the chord's 3rd and sharp 9th degrees. And spicy is a good description for that chord's interval recipe!

THE MAJOR TENTH

Raising the sharp ninth a fret creates the major tenth. I felt braver and stretched a bit here and also found five possibilities starting with this one.

Major 10th

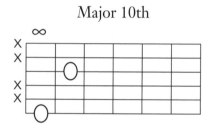

Fig. 2.37. Major Tenth

This interval sounds pretty on this series of open major triads. The major tenth is found between the bottom and top notes of each chord's root and major 3rd degrees. I added an open A string down below as a pedal point or repeated bass note. I ended with a triad plus a 9 added for a little milder splash of spice.

Don't forget the open A string as a pedal point. Also notice the parallel motion of the first three chords—how the fingering is exactly the same.

Let me try it.

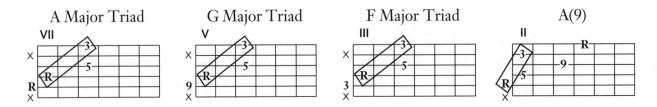

Fig. 2.38. Open Triads with Tenths

That's a really nice finger-style classical touch you added to that progression, Chester.

Thanks. I got it from a Fernando Sor folio.

Great idea.

THE NATURAL ELEVENTH OR SUSPENDED FOURTH

I found five possibilities for the natural eleventh—another dual-personality interval, depending on context. Double labels here, please.

Natural 11th/Suspended 4th

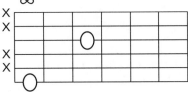

Fig. 2.39. Natural Eleventh/Suspended Fourth

The natural eleventh—a compound perfect fourth, being a half step higher than a major tenth (a compound major third)—has that "Amen" thing and is used for dominant 7sus4 or suspended fourth (11) chords, as well as a gentle tension 11 on minor 7th chords. Here are examples of each.

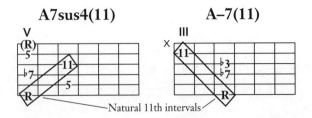

Fig. 2.40. A7sus4(11) and A–7(11)

THE SHARP ELEVENTH (♯11)

I also found five possibilities for the sharp eleventh.

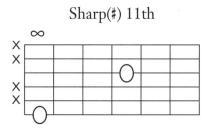

Sharp(♯) 11th

Fig. 2.41. Sharp Eleventh

This is a nice bright interval and sits prettily on major 7th and dominant 7th chords. It is often used to end tunes, especially a nice ballad. Here is an example: an EMaj7(♯11). It has an air of mystique.

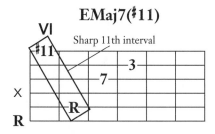

EMaj7(♯11)

Fig. 2.42. EMaj7(♯11)

A light brush with my thumb through this chord produced a pretty effect.

THE TWELFTH

Bringing up the sharp eleventh a fret creates the twelfth, a peaceful but powerful interval, as is its simple complement, the perfect fifth. I wish I could think of something sexy to do with it. Sorry, I am stumped!!

Wait! I found something, Jon! I took the two fingerings for the twelfth illustrated below and played them at the 3rd fret with some open strings. Fingerstyle, folky, and bluegrass grooves all worked.

Thanks for your inspiration with those twelfths, Chester!

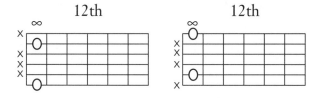

Fig. 2.43. Twelfths

THE FLAT THIRTEENTH (♭13)

Raising the twelfth a fret brings us to the flat thirteen. I found only two possibilities for this interval.

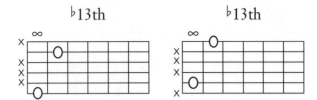

Fig. 2.44. Flat Thirteenths

In certain harmonic situations, this interval will be technically called a sharp fifth. It is often used on dominant 7th chords in which that flat 13th degree very politely and magnetically resolves to the 3rd degree of the restful chord that usually follows it! Here is a simple cadence. Make sure to play that open D string for the CMaj7(9) chord. The open string adds a nice tone color here.

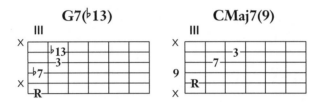

Fig. 2.45. G7($\flat$13) Resolving to CMaj7(9)

THE NATURAL THIRTEENTH

A flat thirteenth brightens up nicely to a natural thirteenth with a one-fret shift. I also found only two possibilities for the natural thirteenth.

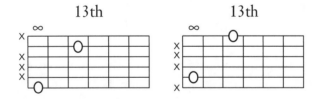

Fig. 2.46. Natural Thirteenths

The thirteenth is a nice bright interval. Here is a simple vamp that illustrates its positive attitude nicely, and that of the natural 9th degree as well: A7(13) to DMaj7(9).

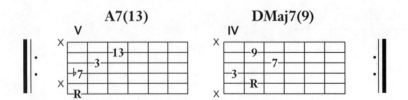

Fig. 2.47. A7(13) to DMaj7(9)

Let's finish up these Dyad/Interval Template sheets for now.

The intervals of the flat and natural thirteenths are essentially the "highest" extensions technically in popular-music harmonic language. As guitarists, we will be using even larger compound intervals. Piano players get really scared when they hear the size of some of our voicings—especially some open-string forms like the EMaj7(♯11) in figure 2.42. The interval between that open E string root of the chord up to that sharp 11th degree is actually two octaves plus an augmented fourth! We can call that interval a sharp nineteenth if we wanted!! Actually, in general music language, it is still considered a humble sharp eleventh. I've actually never heard of a sharp nineteenth until now!

Oh, by the way, we used three template sheets for the Dyad/Interval Forms.

Good, Chester. And thanks for being such a good worker!

Say Jon, what about that Ear Study and the Million Dollar Idea you promised?!

Thanks, Chester, for reminding me.

LEARNING TO HEAR OUR DISCOVERIES: THE MILLION-DOLLAR IDEA

During construction, you will technically and visually learn many harmonic structures, from monads and dyads to 5-part chords and upper-structure triads. It is also very important to learn to recognize these structures with your ear—something like learning bird songs or any other language, for that matter.

Here is one simple study you can try, but first, that *Million Dollar Idea*! I have been an avid bird watcher for about twenty-five years, and one of the most fascinating parts of the sport is learning the bird songs and calls. On the bird-watching market—which is at least a multi-million dollar industry, by the way—there are recordings of bird songs and calls for study purposes. They basically consist of someone saying the name of a bird followed by that bird's song and call, followed immediately by another. Something like this.

"Rose-breasted Grosbeak…" tweety-tweety tweety tweet

"Black-headed Grosbeak…" p'tweety p'tweety ti ti p'tweety

And so on. Now I thought that if the recording was designed so that the song and call came first, followed by the human voice stating the bird species name, then the listener would be an active learner instead of a passive learner.

tweety-tweety tweety tweet "Rose-breasted Grosbeak…"

p'tweety p'tweety ti ti p'tweety "Black-headed Grosbeak…

I can hear the sound and make an assumption followed by an assessment!

Right, Chester!

Now, if you (or I, if I beat you to it) came out with this whole new *revolutionary concept*, we might make a nice pile of cash. Maybe. The reason I share this with you is because we can at least apply this revolutionary new idea to help us learn to hear harmonic structures!

Here is the study.

A CHORD ID STUDY

1. Choose a harmonic structure area for study. For now, let's say dyads, our 2-part chords (intervals).

2. Make a list of all interval possibilities. For reference, copy the chapter 2 interval listing from the Table of Contents.

3. Now make a recording of about thirty minutes in length.

4. In your recording, at random, choose a dyad/interval quality from your reference list, and play that interval anywhere you wish on the fingerboard. Then state with your voice the interval's name. Let the interval continue to sound by re-attacking it. Do this along with a metronome, if you wish. Set the metronome at about 60 beats per minute, and use two beats for the interval and two beats for your voice.

5. Choose another dyad/interval randomly from your reference list. Again, play for two beats, then state the interval name with your voice for two beats.

Try for a thirty-minute long recording, if possible. Remember, choose each interval randomly, since this is training for ear recognition. *Don't cheat!*

When you complete the recording, test yourself. At first, just listen to the tape. Observe. As you gain confidence with recognizing these interval colors and qualities, listen and try a guess. Good luck! Eventually, make other tapes with other harmonic structures as your confidence builds.

If you beat me to it, with my revolutionary *Million Dollar Idea*, at least send me 10 percent!

Here is another study, "An Interval Ear Study," to help with interval recognition. This study brings your voice into play. Making your body an instrument through singing helps us to truly become the music, become the interval—a very sensual experience!

AN INTERVAL EAR STUDY

1. Choose a position area for study.

2. Choose an interval and direction for study. For example, minor thirds ascending.

3. Play a note in the position chosen. *Sing* what you think is a minor third ascending from the note you are playing. Continue playing the first note, creating harmony with your voice. Feel the interval quality in your chest as you sing with the note. Re-attack the note if needed.

4. Now *play* a minor third ascending on your guitar. If you are singing the correct note, good. If not, play the starting note again, and try singing again with your instrument's help.

Continue. Play another note and continue as above. Don't always use the same finger for your starting note, but *stay in that position area*. Give all fingers a chance! Also give all strings a chance for the starting note. This will help your hand learn to play all fingering possibilities for the intervals.

Eventually, identifying intervals by ear will become as easy as color identification is to your eyes. Picturing a hand shape on the fingerboard will help you remember the sound as well.

TRIADS: 3-PART CHORDS

"In our searcheth for the biggest, coolest chord in the world, lest we forget the humble triad?"

—Sir William Shakespeare (Only Kidding!!!)

What could be easier than 3-note chords? Just add another note to any of the dyad/interval forms in chapter 2! That's a lot of possibilities! We will take a look at many types of 3-note chords, with the help of the Palette Chart in "The Roof" chapter, but first, let's explore just one of them—the major triad—and see why this simple humble 3-part chord gets so much attention. Not only is it the foundation of our harmonic system, but also, it is an important element in more complex harmonic concepts such as slash chords (chapter 7). And triads also sound great by themselves, especially when handled by sensitive artists such as you!

Why thank you, Jon!

I was referring to our fellow chord explorers, Chester.

Oops. Sorry.

MOTHER NATURE AT WORK AGAIN

In the world of building chords, there is a hierarchy. This hierarchy is not unlike the taxonomic system of organizing living creatures in which Latin is used to describe from the kingdom all the way to the general (genus) to specific order (species) of a particular creature. In fact, you will feel life within the harmonic motion of the musical examples you play throughout this book. All chords are built from a foundation or "general" note—what is called a root or bottom—from which the other tones of the chord radiate "upwards" sound-wise and structurally, gradually creating a specific chord quality. This root is also called the 1st degree. As we saw in the monad/1-note chord chapter, Mother Nature dictates basic harmonic foundations. The root naturally radiates other tones, the strongest tones creating a subtle (soft) major triad—a 3-part chord. Thanks to Mother Nature, the major triad is the strongest 3-note structure, and proves this by being the veritable foundation of our Western European harmonic system!

WOW! That's impressive!

The major triad consists of three notes, in its basic close-position form: a root note, a major third, and a minor third. It is a pile of thirds—a major third and a minor third—adding up to a perfect fifth between the bottom and top notes. Our harmonic system is also called a tertial system: basically built in thirds.

A baseball game wouldn't quite be a baseball game without the major triad—the opening notes of the American and Canadian National Anthems.

Right, Chester! That is a great memory aid for the major triad.

Let's build one of these humble creatures: a simple, 3-note major triad in *root position*; the root is the bottom note of the triad. Since the degrees will first be built as closely together as possible, it is also said to be in "close position."

First, let's find a root to build from. We can start with any note as a root, but for now, let's start on the note C on the 8th fret of our low E string, and build a C major triad. I will illustrate these examples in traditional notation and tablature, as well as on a chord template.

Root C on Low E String

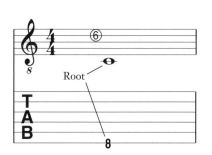

Fig. 3.1. Root of a C Major Triad

Now that we have the root in place, the next note will be the major 3rd degree—the note E natural, since we are building a major type of chord and since it is a major third above the root. It is also the 3rd degree of the C major scale from which the C major triad is built. We will again take a look at the scale as a harmonic building block in the "4-Part Chords" chapter.

Root and 3rd Degree

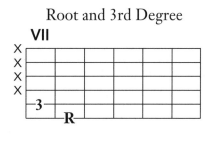

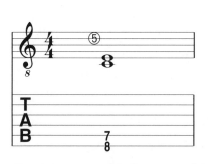

Fig. 3.2. Root and 3rd Degree of C Major Triad

Next, to complete the root-position, close C major triad, the note G natural a perfect fifth above the root is placed above the root and major 3rd degrees.

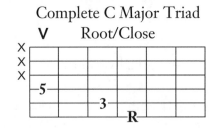

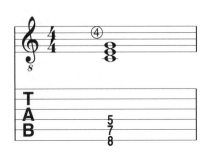

Fig. 3.3. Complete C Major Triad

A simple and solid sound. Obviously, a great foundation to build from.

It sure is, Chester.

One of my most powerful, harmonic experiences was singing with an early 1960s a capella group on the street corners of good old Eastern Parkway, in Brooklyn, New York. We simply sang triadic harmony, and it was a really rich experience. I strongly feel that the human voice is a most special instrument. When singing, our bodies become our instruments, closely touching and being the harmony. Check out "An Interval Ear Study" (chapter 2), a harmonic study using your voice to help create an intimate experience with harmony.

A capella? That sounds like some fancy pasta shape to me.

Actually, a capella refers to a vocal ensemble that does not use instrumental accompaniment, Chet. May I call you Chet?

No way, baby! It's Chester!

Apologies, Chester.

Let's find some of these humble close-position major triad creatures on our fingerboard. This first group will be in root position.

So grab a fresh, blank template sheet, and label it "Major Triads." In the first template, sketch in the major triad in root-position form illustrated in figure 3.3. Label it "Root/Close," since it is the form for a major triad in root and close position.

In your dictionary, you don't need to sketch in the Roman numeral, since this chord form can be played anywhere on this set of strings, depending on the root you choose. I use the infinity sign (∞) to indicate this.

Next, as we did with the dyads/intervals construction, let's find this major triad in root and close position on other string sets. In all, there are four possibilities. I will give you this first set to get you started (see figure 3.4). Observe the intervals at play. In root position, there are a major third and a minor third, creating a perfect fifth between the bottom and top notes. Notice how the form shape changes near the G and B strings, since the interval distance between the adjacent G and B strings is a major third, not a perfect fourth, as with the other adjacent pairs of strings.

Sketch in these four possibilities on the top line of your major triads template sheet.

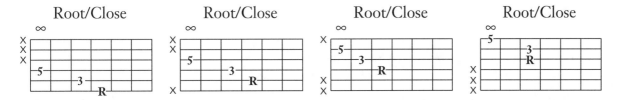

Fig. 3.4. Close Major Triads, All String Sets

Now, let's invert the root-position form. The bottom note, the root, moves up an octave to become the top note, leaving the 3rd degree as the bottom note. This is called "first inversion." Here is the C major triad in root position moving to its first inversion in standard notation. The template shows a first-inversion major-triad form on the bottom three strings.

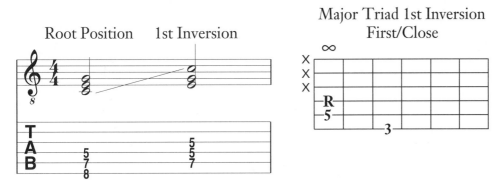

Fig. 3.5. Root Position Moving to First Inversion

Sketch in this first inversion form to start the second line of your Major Triad Template sheet, and label it "First/Close," since it is a major triad in first inversion and close position. Now, find this form on the other string sets, placing them under the root position forms. Don't forget to label them! Observe the intervals at play. In first inversion, there is a minor third between the 3rd and 5th degrees. Then, there is a perfect fourth between the 5th degree and the root, creating a minor sixth between the bottom and top notes.

Now, let's take the first inversion forms and move them to second inversion. The bottom note, the 3rd degree, moves up an octave, to become the top note, making the

5th degree the new bottom note. That's second inversion. In figure 3.6, the C major triad in first inversion moves to second inversion. The template shows a second-inversion major-triad form on the bottom three strings.

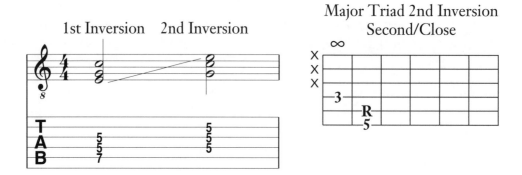

Fig. 3.6. First Inversion Moving to Second Inversion

Sketch in this second inversion form to start the third line of your "Major Triad" Template sheet, and label it "Second/Close," since it is a major triad in second inversion and close position. Now, find these second inversion triad forms on the other string sets, placing them under the first inversion forms. Again, observe the intervals at play. In second inversion, there is a perfect fourth then a major third, creating a major sixth between the bottom and top notes.

If we invert the second inversion, we return to a root position form, which we have sketched in already on the top line!

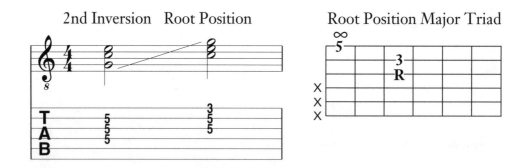

Fig. 3.7. Second Inversion Moving to Root Position

That completes the close-position major-triad forms. You should have three rows: a nice neat pile of twelve close-position major triad possibilities.

Can we use some of these triad guys in action, Jon?

Sure, Chester!

Before we move on to the rich, resonant, open major triads, let's take a brief look at some of these close-position major triads and have a

GLITZY, SPARKLY, CLOSE-POSITION, MAJOR TRIAD SHOW!

On with the show! I mentioned briefly that these humble triads are powerful in themselves. There are thousands of tunes built from major triads alone! And not only national anthems!

The triads are also integral parts of more complex harmonic concepts. Here is a brief peek at some close triads, which are filling an important role as part of some slash chords! More about these guys in chapter 7.

Here is a series of chord forms that consist of the close-position major triads we just built, but now placed over bass notes that make these triads sound Glitzy and Sparkly! These forms are part of the slash chord family. In general chord symbol language, the slash / represents the word "over."

You can play this series of upper structure triads forms in any style or groove you wish. Enjoy listening to them, but also observe the close triad forms (the top three notes **in bold type**) as part of the structures. The Sparkly and Glitzy sound is not only due to the brightness of the major triad on top but also the interval between the bottom notes and some of the triad notes. Look for some of those rich intervals like sevenths and ninths that we met in the "Dyads/Intervals" chapter (chapter 2).

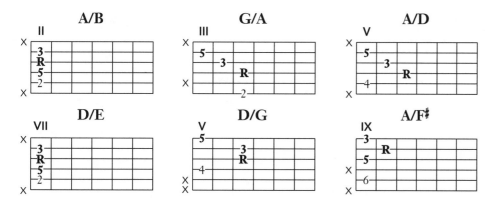

Fig. 3.8. Glitzy Sparkly Slash Chords!

Sounds like a Vegas big band!

I guess you could say that, Chester. I also heard them possibly working in a nice tight fusion groove. And when played slowly and prettily, it might inspire a nice pop ballad. Just add lyrics and a little heat!

Not all slash chords are bright. Some are downright nasty! As we shall see in chapter 7.

THE OPEN-POSITION TRIADS

If you thought the close-position triads were cool, wait until you check out these open-position triads.

We met some open triads back in the Dyads chapter, right Jon?

Yes, Chester, we saw some in action with the major tenth interval.

They are called open-position triads because instead of being triads in close position, they are in open position....

Duh....?

...and open position simply means we are going to open up some space in the close triad by moving the middle note, or voice, up or down an octave.

Since larger intervals are part of these open triad forms, more form possibilities exist. I will again let you know of the possibilities I have found as we proceed with construction.

Figure 3.9 shows the first close-position form we sketched in earlier and one possible open triad form. I am moving the middle voice up an octave so that the open triad will retain its original position—in this case, root position.

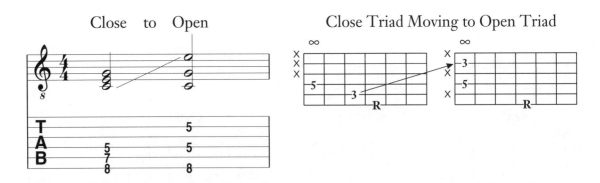

Fig. 3.9. Close Triad Moving to Open Triad

Since open-position forms include larger intervals, more fingering possibilities will open up. Don't be afraid to shift notes to other strings to make room for another possibility. Also, use pure intervallic observation to open up a possible form. Keep the bottom voice on the low E string, for consistency. The intervals of a root-position open major triad are a perfect fifth and a major sixth, creating a major tenth between the bottom and top voices. Notice how inversions and compound intervals appear.

Here are the three possibilities I found. Sketch these in on your Major Triads Template Sheet right after the close forms, and label them "Root/Open."

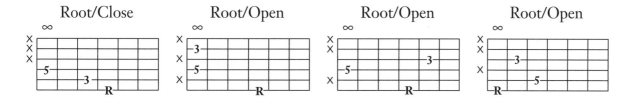

Fig. 3.10. Close Triad Moving to Three Possible Open-Triad Forms

Now, try the next root-position close triad, and find its open possibilities. I found three possibilities here. One was quite a stretch, but it actually produced a new possibility for me. Remember, interval thinking helps. Look for a perfect fifth and a major sixth to help you find a "hidden form."

Continue and find all open possibilities for the rest of the close triads. Some will produce more possibilities than others. In fact, the third root/close triad only produced two forms. The fourth, on the top strings, produced none! As mentioned earlier, bringing the middle voice down an octave also creates an open triad. Doing this with the top set of close triads would produce the forms you have found already. Try it!

Say Jon, what makes open triads sound so rich and powerful?

Good observation, Chester. Since there is more "air" around the notes of an open triad, each note's tone color is heard more distinctly, creating the rich quality. The clarity of the perfect fifth creates the power.

I finished up the rest of those open triads and found two possibilities from each of the first three first inversion forms, but none for the fourth (top string form). The second inversion produced a bit more. I may have missed one. But anyway, I finished the Major Triads Template sheet.

We found twenty possible forms for the open major triads!

Good work, Chester!

BAR CHORDS

Say Jon, where in *tarnation* are those bar chords I've heard about? They're triads, aren't they?

Why yes, some bar chords are triads, Chester!

Basically, the term "bar" refers to when the index finger of our chording hand is held straight, like a bar, to hold down either all six strings (a full bar) or just some of the strings (a half bar), to execute a fingering. Or...

Where do bar chords come from?

Well, sit down, son. Remember earlier, in the "Dyads/Intervals" chapter, we mentioned that when an orchestral work consists of only two parts, those parts are often doubled with unisons and octaves to add strength and more tone colors? On our own private orchestra, the guitar, a bar chord is a good example of this.

To give more support to the triad forms we just found, we can duplicate or double some of the degrees on other strings with octaves. Here are some of the close-triad forms from our major triad template sheet. But now, thanks to the added support of the doubled notes, they have more oomph! A 5- or 6-note chord from a 3-part chord! The original 3-note triad voicing is in bold type for reference.

THE PRINCIPAL MAJOR TRIAD FULL- AND HALF-BAR CHORDS

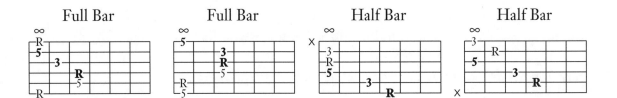

Fig. 3.11. Principal Full- and Half-Bar Chords

Figure 3.11 shows the two principal 6-note full-bar chords and the two principal 5-note half-bar chords for major triads. You can also remove notes from these to make 4- and 5-note triad structures, depending on your needs. Remember that in this dictionary, your vocabulary will always be growing.

One of my first full-bar-chord experiences was with the tune "Tequila," whose rather quick-moving progression consists of a major-triad full-bar chord moving down two frets to another major-triad full-bar chord and then back and forth again, and again and again.... OUCH! The next section of the tune, the bridge, was a blessing for my hand—even though the bridge starts with a diminished chord! It was a much-needed rest from those full-bar chords!

Start a new template sheet and label it "Bar Chords." Add the major-triad forms in figure 3.11 to start your Bar Chords Template. We will use these to next create the bar-chord forms for minor triads, and in chapter 4, we will add some 4-part 7th bar-chord forms. And in chapter 5, some one tension bar-chord forms.

Now, back to 3-part triads.

The 3-part triads come in four different flavors (in music lingo, chord "qualities"): major, minor, diminished, and augmented.

Let's use the major-triad template sheet we just built to help us find those other qualities. First, the Minor Triads Template sheet.

MINOR TRIAD

Chord Degrees: Root, Minor 3rd, Perfect 5th

The minor triad is the "dark side" of the major triad, since the major 3rd degree is lowered a half step. Remember that thanks to Mother Nature, the root note has a major third sounding softly above it as an overtone. When the major 3rd degree of the chord is lowered, a subtle dissonance (rub) is created between that minor 3rd degree and the major 3rd overtone. This is what creates the "dark side" effect. The opening three notes of the theme from *The Godfather* is a close-position minor triad in second inversion. Speaking of the dark side, I wonder what chord was used for Darth Vader's theme?

To create the Minor Triads Template sheet, grab a fresh blank template sheet and label it "Minor Triads." Then copy the major-triad template sheet, but move the major 3rd degree of each template down a half step (one fret) to make it a minor 3rd degree, creating minor triads.

Here is what your first minor-triad template should look like.

First Minor Triad of Template

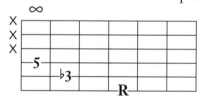

Fig. 3.12. First Minor Triad of Template

Now, on your Bar Chords Template sheet, below the major-triad bar-chord forms, write in the minor-triad bar-chord forms. Notice that the half-bar chord forms don't shift easily to minor and may be impossible to play. Henceforth, don't write them in or try to play any of these! Put them into the dumpster, for now. Try using a friendlier, smaller 4-note variation of these, and sketch those in.

DIMINISHED TRIAD

Chord Degrees: Root, Minor 3rd, Diminished 5th

Grab a fresh template sheet and label it "Diminished Triads." Copy the Minor Triads Template sheet, but lower the perfect fifth degree of each template down a fret to create a diminished 5th degree. Here is what the first diminished-triad form should look like. Watch that stretch! The root position form is tricky with the lowered or diminished 5th degree.

First Diminished Triad of Template

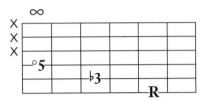

Fig. 3.13. First Diminished Triad of Template

Remember how my first diminished chord experience didn't go so well? When you play some of these diminished guys, you will understand why. I'm doing my Diminished Triads Template sheet on a rainy day! Sob! Since the good old solid perfect 5th degree has been lowered to a diminished 5th, an "instability" has been created. It is a nice effect, actually, and great for those scary movies. "Jason!!!" Maybe even for Darth Vader! They are used often and are great contrasts and transitions to brighter harmonies.

I love *Star Wars*, Jon. I will listen to Darth Vader's theme for what chord quality is used.

Thanks for the research, Chester.

Here is a G diminished triad resolving into a G major triad. Notice the bottom voice's root stays the same (an ostinato), and the top two voices move chromatically upward.

Diminished chords are actually pretty flexible guys, as we will again see later in construction. In fact, you can resolve these diminished triads by moving one or two notes up or down, by step. Find your own possibilities.

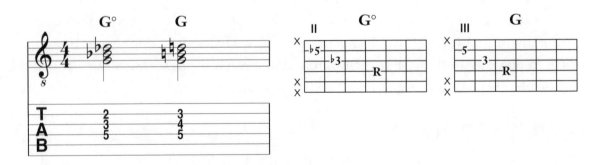

Fig. 3.14. Diminished Triad Resolving to Major Triad

That sounds like the bridge of "Tequila." I have the tune on a Wes Montgomery recording.

You're right, Chester, And as you can see, a relief from those full-bar chords!

The minor bar chords don't easily shift to diminished-triad bar chords, since the perfect fifth is held under the bar finger. And thank goodness. That would really be depressing.

AUGMENTED TRIAD

Chord Degrees: Root, Major 3rd, Augmented 5th

The last triad flavor, augmented, is simply the major triad with a sharp 5th degree or augmented 5th. Grab another fresh template sheet, label it "Augmented Triads," and then copy the Major Triads Template sheet information except raise the perfect 5th degree of each template up a fret or half a step to create the Augmented Triads Template.

First Augmented Triad of Template

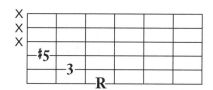

Fig. 3.15. First Augmented Triad of Template

Since the stability of the perfect fifth has again been disturbed, this chord has an active, in-motion quality. Here is a G augmented triad resolving into a C minor triad. Again, find your own possible resolutions.

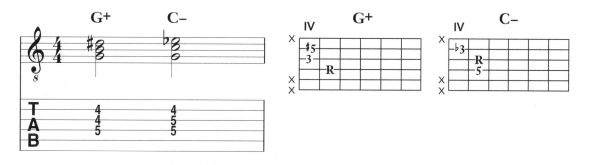

Fig. 3.16. Augmented Triad Resolving to Minor Triad

The introduction of Stevie Wonder's classic hit "You Are the Sunshine of My Life" is a classic example of augmented triads in action.

How about the opening tornado scene from *The Wizard of Oz?!*

They would certainly work for that scene, Chester.

We have now completed a major stage of construction: the major, minor, diminished, and augmented triad template sheets, and the triad bar-chords template sheet. Triads are wonderful sounds in themselves and are also important building blocks for the 4-part 7th chords, which we will build in chapter 4. For now, let's call this family of triads the Traditional or Tertial Triad Family—the basis for our tertial harmonic system.

Working with the power of triads is fun. To close up this chapter, here are the triads I used in composing the opening of a brass trio: two trumpets and a trombone. Play it, and feel the majesty that the triads evoke.

Remember that all of the chords in your dictionary will also work for your composing and arranging work!

BRASS TRIO

Fig. 3.17. Brass Trio

Remember how, in *The Guitarist's Guide to Composing and Improvising,* you showed that flexible, 3-note chords can be used to create counterpoint?

Thank you, Chester. And thanks for the plug.

In chapter 4 of my first book, I use the traditional triad family in close and open forms and in all four flavors to create interesting counterpoint from chord to chord.

Here is the "Brass Trio," but now with a bit of counterpoint added. Basically, I am using simple approach notes from above or below the triad notes. The black circle is the approach note moving in the arrow direction—a brief testament to the physical flexibility of 3-note chord structures. Try having the approach note rhythmically move by itself as the other two notes sustain.

"BRASS TRIO" WITH APPROACHES

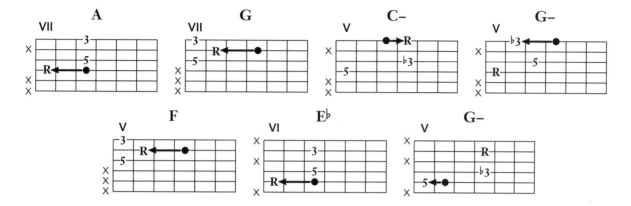

Fig. 3.18. Brass Trio with Approaches

I used that classical-like finger-style pattern with the "Brass Trio" excerpt and it worked well.

Good, Chester.

Now, there are other families of triads or 3-part chords we will explore. There's the Quartal Family Triads (triads built in fourths), and there's the Cluster Family (triads built in seconds). Larger 4-, 5-, and 6-part chords can also be slimmed down to 3-note structures.

That's a lot of possibilities, and it sounds exciting! All these harmonic colors. Let's meet the other families, Jon!

Not quite yet, Chester.

In chapter 9, we will take a look at the Palette Chart. To organize all of these different triad family possibilities, I developed this chart as a visual display of all the triad colors. The triads are organized intervallically and by families. If you wish to take a peek, go ahead (see figure 9.1). But come right back. We have a lot more building to do!

Don't forget to also try the "Million-Dollar Idea Ear Study" (see p. 57) with all qualities of chord structures. Try it with triads. Fourth floor please, Chester.

CHAPTER 4: FOURTH FLOOR

4-PART CHORDS: FOUNDATION FORMS

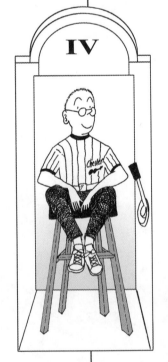

Roughly 87.7 percent of our guitar careers are spent as accompanists (supporting others). Much of that time is spent playing chords—one little pile of about four or five notes moving to another little pile of four or five notes. As supportive guitarists, we should love this technique, since it is our basic bread and butter. When these larger chords are combined with other accompaniment textures, such as dyads, single-note counter lines, various triad families, and 2-part counterpoint, our accompaniment technique takes on another level of possibility.

A CRASH COURSE

Here in "Foundation Forms," we will create a nice collection of 4-part chords—a beautiful family of chord forms, which will serve as a foundation for exploring 5- and 6-part chords. We will work from a template sheet that consists of forty forms for a 4-part major 7th chord. The major 7th chord is simply our nice major triad with a little company: a 7th degree (in this case, a major 7th).

Let's meet one.

Remember I mentioned my reaction to my first major 7th chord. Did I say "heavenly?" Well, here is that very chord form—that open-string form. I almost feel like I am showing an old family photo. Sniff . . . Sniff . . . Play it softly now . . . gently.

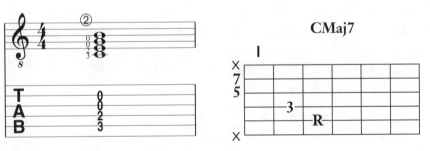

Fig. 4.1. CMaj7 Root Position Close Voicing

Now tune that gitbox, Chester! Try it again. Ain't it sweet?

It sure is, Jon, and those open strings!

Nice beret, Chester!

Thanks, Jon.

This CMaj7 chord is a textbook perfect example of a 4-part major 7th chord in close position, since it is simply adding a fourth part or voice to the C major triad's root, major 3rd, and perfect 5th. A major 7th! As you can see, it's another interval of a third piled on top—the tertial system at work!

Since this section is a crash course in 4-part harmony, let's look at our chord-form construction from another view: a scale-wise view. Let's take a C major scale and pile some thirds on top of each degree. Pile just two thirds for now, creating traditional triads.

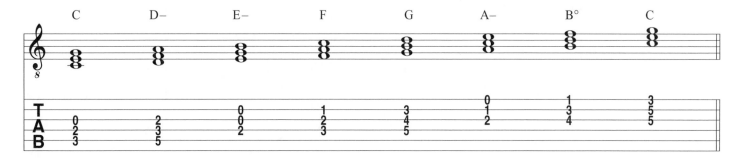

Fig. 4.2. C Major Scale Diatonic Triads

These are the diatonic (in the key) triads in the key of C major, each in root position. Notice the different triad qualities created, since sometimes there are major thirds or minor thirds at play.

Now, let's add another third on top. This creates 4-part 7th chords in the key of C major. Observe the qualities of these chords.

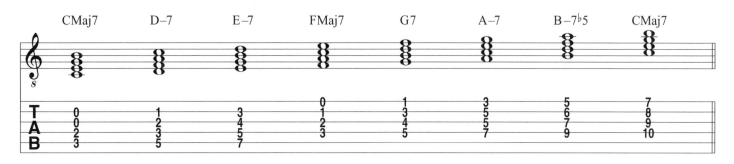

Fig. 4.3. C Major Scale 4-Part 7th Chords

Each major scale has the same set of 4-part 7th chord qualities; only the roots change as the key changes! Try to play the above close-position 7th chords.

Those are *tough* to play, Jon!

They sure are, Chester.

DROP TECHNIQUE

In fact, let's change key to the key of G and talk about the drop concept—a concept that will make life easier for us, since it makes grabbing some of these close-position chords much easier.

Here is a G major 7th chord—another nice pretty sound. This chord is also in close position—root, major 3rd, perfect 5th, and major 7th—and not too hard to play.

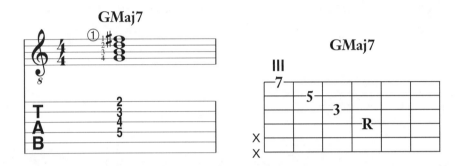

Fig. 4.4. GMaj7 Close Position

I just have to tell you, Chester, that the shape of this chord form sitting on that fingerboard has always visually reminded me of a line of laundry hanging out in the good old Brooklyn sun.

You need to take a break, Jon. I'm gonna work on the Chord Symbol CrossTones Puzzle in the "Break" chapter. I really need work on my chord spelling!

Just a minute, Chester. Let me tell you about the drop concept first, to help with those close 4-part 7th chords.

Now, that GMaj7 chord form is easy to grab.

But! If we wanted to change this major 7th chord form into another simple 4-part chord relative—let's say a minor 7th chord—things may be too close for comfort! Watch what happens. To create this minor 7th quality, we must lower the major 7th degree and the major 3rd degree of the major 7th chord one fret (a half step). Here it is. What a stretch!

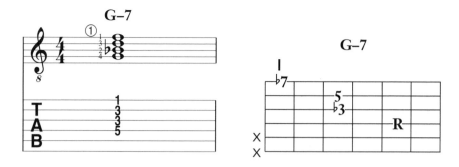

Fig. 4.5. G–7 Close Position

And what if we needed to flatten the 5th degree? Things would be worse!

So, sometimes close-position 4-part 7th and 6th chords may be possible, but most of the time they are impossible!

This is where the drop concept comes in. Let's try shifting some degrees around to see what happens. Here is the minor seventh chord, but now, the root and flat 7 have changed places. This arrangement is much more hand friendly. You can play it using just one finger, and it is still a G–7 chord.

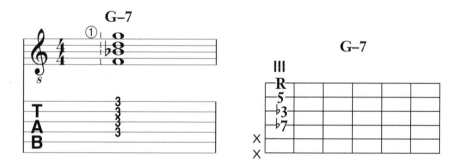

Fig. 4.6. G–7 Drop Technique

These shiftings make for easier playing, and they also sound good, which is a nice combination.

You bet, Chester. This is the drop technique: degrees are dropped from their original close positions to create "drop" chords.

Let's see how drop technique works. In figure 4.7, CMaj7 is illustrated in close-position second inversion (the 5th degree is the bottom or bass note) and then in drop 2 form. Drop 2 means that the second voice of a close-position chord, or the chord's second note from the top is dropped an octave. In this example, the root note C is the second voice and dropped an octave. The standard notation example is much easier to look at to study this process.

In drop 2 position, Ooo La Laaaaahhhh!!! (That was French, Chester.) The root is now dropped to the bottom voice.

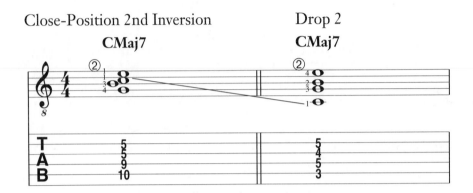

Fig. 4.7. CMaj7 in Close-Position Second Inversion

Now, I just have to show you a drop form of the GMaj7 chord we played earlier. It is officially a "drop 2 & 4" chord form. I call it the "Tony Mottola" chord, since that is from whom I learned it—one of the great guitarists. I probably saw him playing this monster chord on the old Johnny Carson *Tonight Show*. It is quite a reach, so don't hurt yourself. In fact, bring it way up the fretboard, and try it. Here it is as a GMaj7 chord.

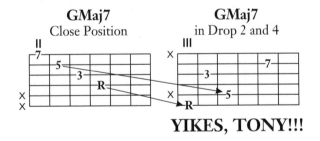

YIKES, TONY!!!

Fig. 4.8. GMaj7 in Drop 2 & 4 Position

I hope this crash course in harmony and drop technique helped. Details of chord qualities will be given to help in the construction process! Grab your hard hat, and let's get going!

Photocopy the Major 7 Template (see figure 4.9), and put it in your binder with the completed dyad and traditional triad templates. We will use this template as a foundation to build the rest of the 4-part chord qualities.

We will construct fifteen different qualities of 4-part chords. These 4-part chord forms are great sounds in themselves and will also be a good staging or base for the tension work construction in chapter 5, "5-Part Chords."

On the Major 7 Template are forty different forms for major 7th chords, in different inversions and drop forms. Each row, except for the bottom row, starts with a major 7th chord in root position, in a particular drop form (indicated on the Template sheet), followed by its first, second, and third inversions staying on the same string set. Drop 2, drop 3, drop 2 & 4, and drop 2 & 3 possibilities are included. The bottom row consists of four possible close-position major 7th chord forms: two in root position and two in first inversion.

When we build any new chord quality template, I will describe its chord quality, list its chord degrees, and discuss how to create this new chord quality, relative to a template already completed. I will often include a simple musical example using that chord quality, so that you can see it and play it in action. The first chord template of each new quality will be given, to help you get started with a new template sheet.

Hold it, Jon! I tried that last row of the Major 7 Template, and two of them are finger busters!

I know, Chester. They are included because as we move through other chord qualities, shifting degrees, these forms will become easier to grab, depending on the particular quality. I stopped at this group of forty. It is enough for now!

I'll say!

As the construction process continues, you will find many duplications of chord-form shapes. These duplications are called *enharmonic equivalents*—the same notes with different chord names. It's like getting two or three chords for the price of one! I will point many of these out for you in the enharmonic look-alikes section of each chord quality introduction. There, the acronym "AR" is used to describe the term *assumed root*, which indicates that the root of the original chord quality is not present in the enharmonic look-alike. Also used is the term *slash chord*, which refers to a chord symbol such as C/D, in which the slash is used to indicate that a C major triad is placed over a D bass note. Do not let these technicalities bog down the construction process! Keep going. A more in-depth look at these terms will be taken in the "5-Part Chords" chapter and the "Slash Chords" chapter.

THE MAJOR 7 TEMPLATE

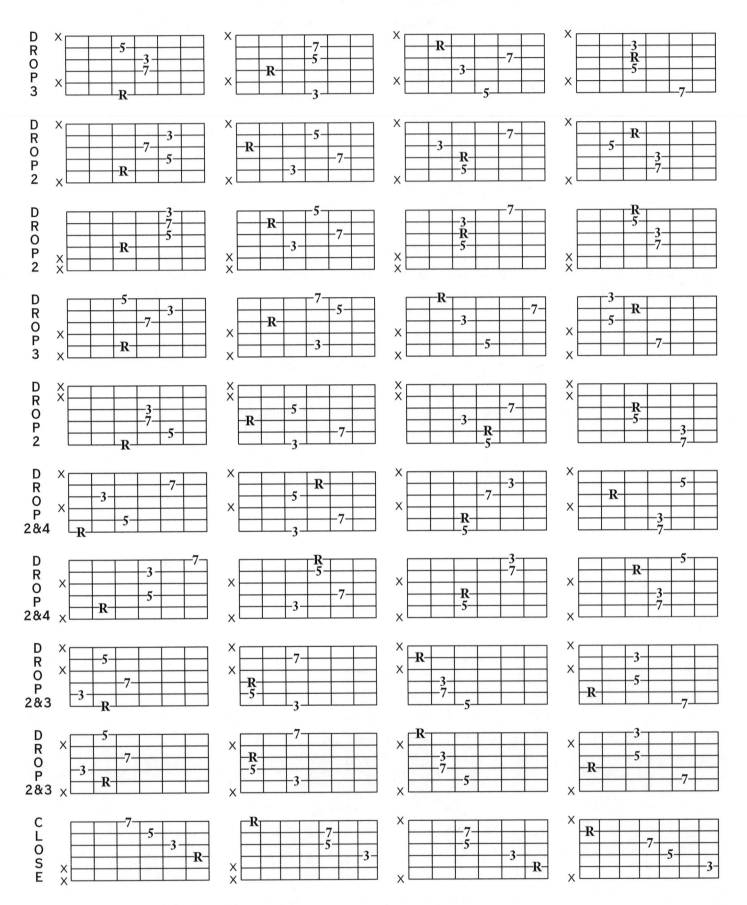

Fig. 4.9. Major 7 Template

The basic order of construction for the 4-part chord qualities will be first the major qualities, followed by the dominant 7th qualities, the minor qualities, and then the diminished 7th qualities. I will also make note of some common chord symbol alternatives for each quality of 4-part chord (see p. 14).

Again, if a chord form or fingering is totally impossible to play, it may become possible later. Degrees will shift as we will explore other qualities.

You may notice that in shifting a degree to create a new chord quality, the degree "falls out" of the fingerboard template. Simply move the starting form over a fret or two to make room for this new degree. On the starter Major 7th Chord Form Template, the forms are centered to allow for this expansion and contraction.

During construction, you will find voicings that are "meat and potatoes" chords, which you will use regularly in your playing. You will also find very unusual configurations. This can be a good thing. Use the uniqueness of the voicing to inspire a new musical direction. Remember that the chord vocabulary we are developing here is to be used to meet our musical needs not only as guitarists performing particular idioms but also as inspirational catalysts for our creative musical endeavors. Even if I use a particular voicing only once to stimulate a composition or serve as a refreshing alternative to the "status quords," I am happy.

How do I remember all these chords, Jon?!

As with any language, Chester, understanding the context of a word is important to create a connection.

The same is true in music harmonic language, and this is why I have included many hands-on examples for folks to play and see (hear) how chords work together, and why.

You're the cat, Jon!

Me-oow!

Here we go, Chester. Grab that Major 7 Template, and copy some blank templates to get us started. You will find them in the "Tool Box," chapter 14.

MAJOR 7

Chord Degrees: Root, Major 3rd, Perfect 5th, Major 7th

Common Symbols: CMaj7, CMa7, C∆7, C△7

The given Major 7th Chord Form Template sheet will get us started. Here is the first chord form given on the Major 7th Chord Template provided. For each new chord form quality introduced, I will illustrate the first chord and then leave the rest of the sheet up to you.

Major 7

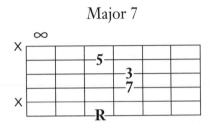

Fig. 4.10. First Major 7 Template Form

Major 7 is a very common, pretty chord quality. As you know, I can still remember the first one I played! I'll use that very first close-position form in context when I introduce the next chord quality, the major 7♯5 chord.

Enharmonic Look-Alikes

The major 7th chord quality is enharmonic with minor 7(9). So C major 7 is enharmonic with an A minor 7(9) chord. It is enharmonic with some slash chords: E–/C and C/B. If you remember, a slash chord is a chord symbol that uses a slash to represent the word "over." So E–/C is an E minor triad over the note C, and C/B is a C major triad over the note B. Go to the "7th Floor" for a closer peek, if you wish.

MAJOR 7♯5

Chord Degrees: Root, Major 3rd, Sharp 5th, Major 7th

Common Symbols: CMaj7♯5, CMaj7(+5), C+Maj7, C△7♯5

Let's dive in the pool and create a Major 7♯5 Template sheet. Grab a blank template, and label it at the top, Major 7♯5. Copy everything from the provided Major 7 template sheet except move the 5th degree up (to the right) a half step (one fret) to ♯5. Your first chord diagram of the Major 7♯5 sheet should look like figure 4.11. Complete the rest of the Major 7♯5 sheet.

First Major 7♯5 Template Form

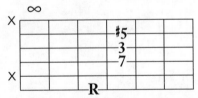

Fig. 4.11. First Major 7♯5 Template Form

I first heard this chord quality in action from Tony Mottola in a guitar solo arrangement he played of the classic ballad "*Misty*." Or as the guy at the gig drunkenly requests, "Hey do you guys know 'Look at Me?'" Tony used the major 7♯5 chord as an approach chord to a regular major 7th chord. In this sequence below, I begin with an E♭Maj7♯5 chord, which moves to an E♭Maj7. Notice the sharp 5th degree moving down to the natural 5th degree. The sequence ends with the sharp 5th degree of the A♭Maj7♯5 chord moving *up* chromatically to the 6th degree of the A♭Maj7(6) chord.

Both effects are pretty. If you don't know the melody of "Look at Me," have your Uncle Tony sing it to you.

You don't want to hear my Uncle Tony sing!

If that's the case, the progression sounds pretty all by itself, also.

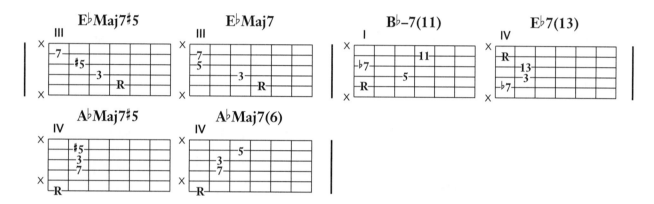

Fig. 4.12. Maj7♯5 "Misty"

This harmonic cliché has been used in many tunes, and it works as an introduction or even a nice vamp to jam over. Use it in any key or with any rhythmic groove you wish, from ska to swing. And, of course, try different chord forms. The example in figure 4.13 is just one possibility. This nice, simple close-position form works nicely here as a foundation.

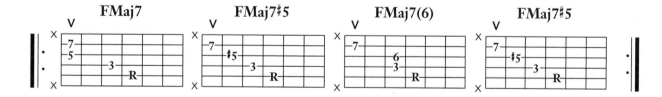

Fig. 4.13. Maj7♯5 Cliché

I feel a lot of power in this progression, but I only see one note, the 5th degree, moving chromatically.

A little motion, Chester, but a lot of power and depth, which comes from a combination of the chromatic motion contrasting against the repeated notes.

Enharmonic Look-Alikes

The Maj7#5 chord is enharmonic with the slash-chord major triad over its raised 5th. So, CMaj7#5 is enharmonic with an E/C chord. The CMaj7#5 chord is also enharmonic with an A–Maj7(9) chord.

MAJOR 7♭5

Chord Degrees: Root, Major 3rd, Lowered 5th, Major 7th

Common Symbols: CMaj7♭5, CMaj7(–5), C△7♭5

Major 7♭5 is a popular sound more commonly written as Maj7(#11). A classic usage is as a possible starting chord quality for "Blue in Green," the Jazz classic, and as a nice touch to end a tune.

Grab another blank template and create a Major 7♭5 sheet. Copy the Major 7 sheet, except now lower the 5th degree one fret (half a step) to ♭5. Here is the first template for this chord.

First Major 7♭5 Template Form

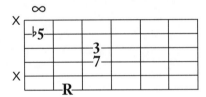

Fig. 4.14. First Major 7♭5 Template Form

Enharmonic Look-Alikes

The major 7♭5 chord is also called major 7(#11), so CMaj7♭5 may be used for CMaj7(#11), which is enharmonic with an **AR** A–6(9), an **AR** D7(9,13), and an **AR** A♭7(#9,♭13).

MAJOR 6

Chord Degrees: Root, Major 3rd, Perfect 5th, Major 6th

Common Symbols: CMaj6 or C6

The major 6th chord quality is a cool retro sound sometimes frowned upon in more modern musical circles. I just listened to some great Duke Ellington, and that band sure made that major sixth sound beautiful. It can be the perfect touch harmonically for its simplicity, especially next to the biggest baddest chord in town. To create this simple harmonic gem, take the 7th degree of the major 7th chord sheet, and lower it two frets down to the 6th degree.

First Major 6 Template Form

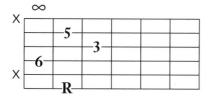

Fig. 4.15. First Major 6 Template Form

Enharmonic Look-Alikes

The major 6th chord is enharmonic with minor 7th chords. So, a CMaj6 chord is also an A–7th chord. It is also enharmonic with an **AR** D7sus 4(9) and an **AR** F Maj7(9).

DOMINANT 7

Chord Degrees: Root, Major 3rd, Perfect 5th, Flat 7th

Common Symbol: C7

Dominant 7th is perhaps the most-used chord quality, since this chord can function as a restful sound as in a blues, or as a powerful transitional chord in a II V I progression. Simply move the 7th degree of the major 7th chord down one fret (a half step) to the flat 7th degree.

First Dominant 7 Template Form

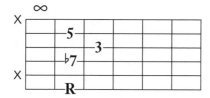

Fig. 4.16. First Dominant 7 Template Form

This chord will be a strong contender in the "Chord Symbol Academy Awards," where the most popular, oft-used chord symbols win big prizes for helping us out the most—see chapter 11, "The Research and Development Lab."

Enharmonic Look-Alikes

Every dominant 7th chord has its alter ego—another dominant 7th chord that is its enharmonic equivalent. C7 is enharmonic with an **AR** G♭7♭5(♭9).

DOMINANT 7♯5

Chord Degrees: Root, Major 3rd, Raised 5th, Flat 7th

Common Symbols: C7♯5 or C7+5

Take the Dominant 7 sheet, and raise the 5th degree up a fret to ♯5 to create the dominant 7♯5 quality.

First Dominant 7♯5 Template Form

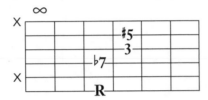

Fig. 4.17. First Dominant 7♯5 Template Form

The dominant 7♯5 quality creates a nice chromatic cadence into a I chord. In the following classic II V I progression, note how the ♯5 of the B♭7♯5 chord (the note F♯) creates a chromatic line that bridges the root of the F–7 chord (the note F) to the 3rd degree of the E♭Maj7 chord (the note G). This E♭Maj7 voicing has a doubling of the 3rd degree—a nice sound.

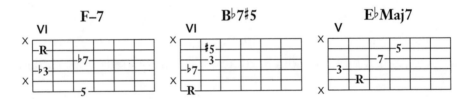

Fig. 4.18. F–7 B♭7♯5 E♭Maj7

Enharmonic Look-Alikes

The dominant 7♯5 chord can also be called dominant 7(♭13). C7♯5 is also enharmonic with an **AR** G♭7(9,♯11) chord.

DOMINANT 7♭5

Chord Degrees: Root, Major 3rd, Lowered 5th, Flat 7th

Common Symbols: C7♭5, C7–5

Take the dominant 7 sheet and *lower* the 5th degree one fret to ♭5, creating the dominant 7♭5 quality.

First Dominant 7♭5 Template Form

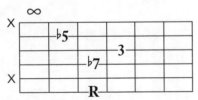

Fig. 4.19. First Dominant 7♭5 Template Form

This powerful sound is often used as a closing chord in jazz tunes and also as part of II V I cadences. Here in figure 4.20, the lowered 5th degree of the G7♭5 moves nicely up a half step to the 9th degree of the I chord, the CMaj7(9).

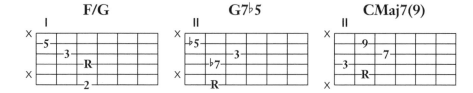

Fig. 4.20. F/G G7♭5 CMaj7(9)

I really like those chromatically moving lines!

As you notice, I do too, Chester!

Enharmonic Look-Alikes

A dominant 7♭5 chord can also be called dominant 7(♯11). C7♭5 is also enharmonic with an **AR** G♭7♭5, an **AR** D7(9,♭13), and an **AR** A♭7(9,♭13).

DOMINANT 7SUS4

Chord Degrees: Root, Perfect 4th, Perfect 5th, Flat 7th

Common Symbols: C7sus4, C7(11)

A classic appearance of the dominant 7sus4 chord is as the opening strum of the Beatles tune "A Hard Day's Night." The sus4 chord symbol means that the 3rd degree is raised (or "suspended") a half step (one fret) to the 4th degree. So, take the Dominant 7 Template sheet and raise the 3rd degree accordingly to create your Dominant 7sus4 Template sheet.

First Dominant 7sus4 Template Form

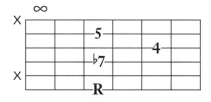

Fig. 4.21. First Dominant 7sus4 Template Form

The 4th degree is "suspended" because it often resolves back down to the 3rd degree. The dominant 7sus4 chord is also complete in itself; Herbie Hancock's tune "Maiden Voyage" is a good example, since every chord is a dominant 7sus4!

Say, Jon, I found some nice new sounds building that Dominant 7sus4 Template. Listen to this one; the B♭Maj7 fingering is a little tough, but worth it.

I know, Chester, the new possibilities continue to appear with our explorations. That fingering will get easier, the more you use it.

Let's take a look and listen to your find.

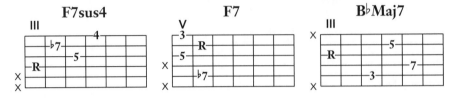

Fig. 4.22. Chester's Dominant 7sus4 Example

A nice example of a dominant 7sus4 in action, Chester. The top voice has the suspended 4th degree resolving to the 3rd degree in the F7 chord. And the bottom voice, or bass note, descends nicely from the root of the F7sus4 chord to the flat 7th degree of F7 to the 3rd degree of B♭Maj7. Nice voice leading!

Voice leading?

Voice leading refers to how you move the degrees of one chord to another.

MINOR 7

Chord Degrees: Root, Minor 3rd, Perfect 5th, Flat 7th

Common Symbols: C–7, CMin7, Cmin7

To create the Minor 7 Template sheet, take the Dominant 7 sheet and lower the 3rd degree a half step (one fret) from a major 3rd to a minor 3rd.

First Minor 7 Template Form

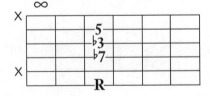

Fig. 4.23. First Minor 7 Template Form

This chord quality might also qualify for a Chord Symbol Academy Award, along with dominant 7. It's tough to find a tune without one.

Enharmonic Look-Alikes

As stated before, minor 7th chords and major 6th chords are enharmonic. C–7 is the same as E♭Maj6. Also, major 7(9) chords, without their roots, look like minor 7th chords. So C–7 looks like **AR** A♭Maj7(9) and the slash chord C–/B♭.

MINOR 7♯5

Chord Degrees: Root, Minor 3rd, Raised 5th, Flat 7th

Common Symbols: C–7♯5, Cmin7♯5

As the Minor 7♯5 symbol implies, take the Minor 7 template sheet and raise the fifth up a half step.

First Minor 7♯5 Template Form

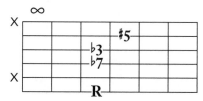

Fig. 4.24. First Minor 7♯5 Template Form

The minor 7♯5 quality is a pretty sound and can also be looked at as a major triad with an added 9th degree in first inversion. Try using an E–7♯5 to fill in for a C triad, sometime. Mellow. Here is a simple cadence using this chord. In this progression, the E–7♯5 is a restful sound and the FMaj7 chord is a gentle bit of action.

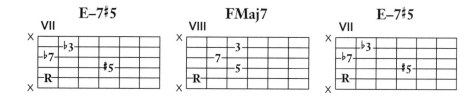

Fig. 4.25. E–7♯5 FMaj7 E–7♯5 Progression

As I was playing the progression, I experimented with making the FMaj7 form an open-string chord form by removing the 7th degree and using an open G string instead. This creates an F major triad with an added 9 (the note G), which works nicely with the color of the E–7♯5. Here is my open-string discovery.

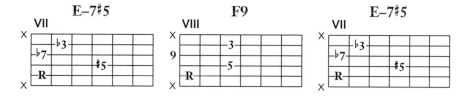

Fig. 4.26. E–7♯5 F(9) E–7♯5 Progression

Much more about open-string chord forms on the Eighth Floor, where I will also show you, in my estimation, the most beautiful chord in the world.

Pssssst! Show me now, Jon, please?

Patience, Chester.

Enharmonic Look-Alikes

Minor 7♯5 is enharmonic with a first inversion major triad with an added 9th degree. So C–7♯5 is similar to **AR** A♭(9) in first inversion.

MINOR MAJOR 7

Chord Degrees: Root, Minor 3rd, Perfect 5th, Major 7th

Common Symbols: C–Maj7, Cmin△7, C–△7, C–⁷.

You can think of this as a major 7th chord with its 3rd lowered a half step (one fret) to ♭3, or you can think of it as minor 7th with its ♭7 raised up a half step to natural or major 7. It's up to you. Both roads lead to a minor major 7th chord.

First Minor-Major 7 Template Form

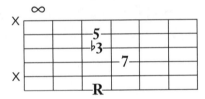

Fig. 4.27. First Minor-Major 7 Template Form

You've heard this classic chord quality tons of times, from Mary Poppins to Duke Ellington, as in this next example. Notice the root on the G string as it moves down by half steps to create the next chord quality. The sequence ends with a minor 6th chord, which is the chord quality coming up next. Notice the open low E string functioning as the root throughout this example. This progression is called a *descending minor cliché*.

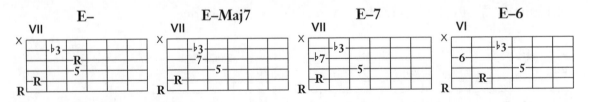

Fig. 4.28. E Minor Descending Cliché

It's tough shifting from the E–7 to the E–6 fingering. I feel like a human pretzel!

When moving from E–Maj7 to E–7, simply lift your middle finger so that fingers 3 and 4 are stationary as you move to the E–6.

Thanks. That helps a lot, Jon.

Working out efficient fingerings is half the battle on this instrument.

By the way, I listened to Darth Vader's theme. It is in minor!

Thanks again for your research, Chester.

Enharmonic Look-Alikes

The only look-alike I can think of is a slash chord E♭+/C for a C–Maj7.

MINOR 6

Chord Degrees: Root, Minor 3rd, Perfect 5th, Major 6th

Common Symbols: Cmin6 or C–6

The minor 6th chord quality is so cool and bluesy thanks to the tritone, or sharp fourth, between the ♭3rd and 6th degrees. Create the Minor 6 Template sheet by taking your Minor 7 sheet and lowering the ♭7 degree down a half step (one fret) to the 6th degree.

First Minor 6 Template Form

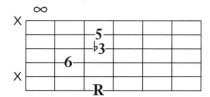

Fig. 4.29. First Minor 6 Template Form

My first minor 6 experience was with the pretty bossa nova "Corcovado," composed by Antonio Carlos Jobim. I will use the minor 6 chord quality in context with the next chord quality, minor 7♭5.

Enharmonic Look-Alikes

Here is a can of worms! You will soon see that the forms on your minor 6 sheet look exactly like the forms on your minor 7♭5 sheet and like many of the forms on your dominant 7(9) sheet coming up in the next chapter. So C–6 looks lots like an A–7♭5, which looks lots like an **AR** F7(9) and an **AR** B7(♭9,♭13).

Whew!!!

MINOR 7♭5

Chord Degrees: Root, Minor 3rd, Flat 5th, Flat 7th

Common Symbols: C–7♭5, Cmin7♭5, Cø

The minor 7♭5 chord is also called "half-diminished," since it is almost a diminished 7th chord—but not quite. As the chord symbol implies, take your minor 7 sheet and lower the 5th degree down a half step to ♭5.

First Minor 7♭5 Template Form

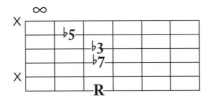

Fig. 4.30. First Minor 7♭5 Template Form

This is an oft-used quality primarily as a II chord in a II V I cadence in minor tonalities, but it is also effective as part of a II V I in major. Here is a II V I in G minor.

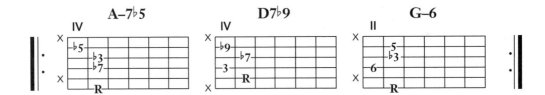

Fig. 4.31. II V I in Minor

Another typical but pretty usage for the minor 7♭5 chord is for endings, as in this chromatic-moving (the bass motion is moving down in half steps) progression, here in the key of C.

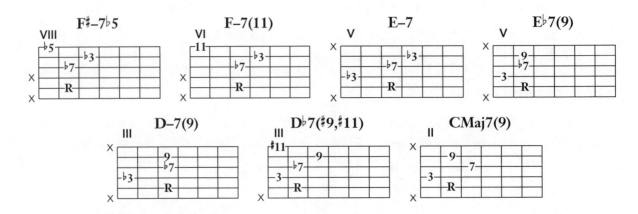

Fig. 4.32. Minor 7♭5 for Ending

I like the ease of hand motion of those voicings and the power of the chromatic line downward. Nice gravitational stuff!

Some of the nicest ideas can be very hand friendly.

Enharmonic Look-Alikes

See the minor 6 chord's look-alikes for the gruesome details.

DIMINISHED 7

Chord Degrees: Root, Minor 3rd, Flat 5th, Diminished 7th(°7)

Common Symbols: C°7, Cdim7

Now let's go all the way, and take the previous "half-diminished" or minor 7♭5 chord and lower its flat 7th degree down a half step (one fret) to create a °7 (diminished seventh) to make it officially a fully diminished 7th chord.

First Diminished 7 Template Form

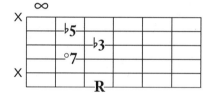

Fig. 4.33. First Diminished 7 Template Form

This is that chord form that let me down, the first time I played it. It didn't sound purdy, but I soon learned that it works great as a transitional chord connecting the pretty stuff. Here are some diminished 7th chords in action.

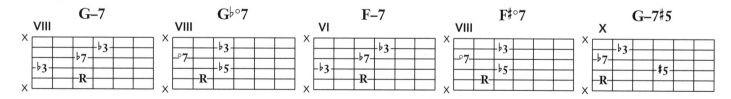

Fig. 4.34. Diminished 7th Chords in Action

Enharmonic Look-Alikes

Diminished 7th chords are symmetrically built; there is a minor third interval between each chord degree. So, the chord shape, when moved up three frets, is still the same chord, or it can be called by any of the other chord tones! So, C°7 is also E♭°7, G♭°7, and A°7. In chapter 5, we will see that when we build dominant 7(♭9) chords, some forms without roots will look *exactly* like the diminished 7th shapes you are creating here.

Another Whew!!

Bless you, Chester.

I didn't sneeze!

DIMINISHED MAJOR 7

Chord Degrees: Root, Minor 3rd, Flat 5th, Major 7th

Common Symbol: C°Maj7, CdimMaj7, Cdim△7, C°7̄.

The easiest way to build the next sheet for diminished major 7 is to copy the Diminished 7th sheet but simply bring the ♭♭7(diminished 7th degree) up a whole step or two frets to the natural 7th (a.k.a. major 7) degree.

First Diminished Major 7 Template Form

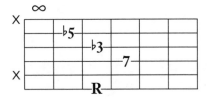

Fig. 4.35. First Diminished Major 7 Template Form

Like the major 7♯5 chord, the diminished major 7th chord quality is a nice approach chord to a regular major 7th chord. One of the first times I heard this effect used was in a tune called "Spring Is Here."

S p r i n g..!

Enough, Chester!!! I shouldn't have encouraged you!

Here is just one of many possible resolutions of this interesting chord quality. This A°Maj7 voicing is a good example of a previously impossible close-position voicing becoming possible through a shifting of degrees.

Fig. 4.36. Spring Is Here

In official harmonic language, the above progression is an example of a tonic diminished chord in action. The diminished chord has the tonic note of the key as its root—in this case, the key of A.

Enharmonic Look-Alikes

The diminished major 7th chord is like one of those slash-chord types, namely the major triad over its lowered 9th degree. So C°Maj7 looks like a B/C chord. More about these guys in the "Slash Chords" chapter. C°Maj7 is also enharmonic with an **AR** A♭7(♯9) and an **AR** D7(♭9,13).

Say Jon, you mentioned something about 7th chords as bar chords back in the "Triads" chapter.

Thanks for the reminder, Chester.

FULL-BAR 4-PART 7TH CHORDS

Here are the most common full-bar chord possibilities for 4-part 7th chords. I'll point out some 1-tension bar-chord possibilities on the Fifth Floor, coming right up.

Can we include this diminished 7th bar chord I found?

Of course, Chester.

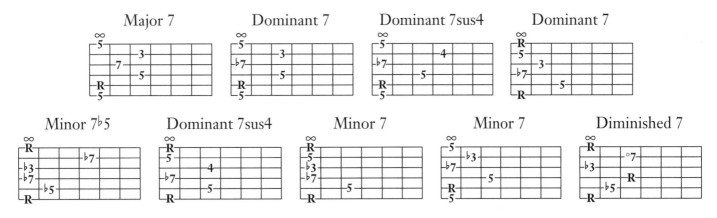

Fig. 4.37. Full-Bar 4-Part 7th Chords

As with all voicings, bar chords have their own distinct personalities. They have a strength due to the doubling of degrees. This creates octaves and puts all six strings in use, creating a fullness of sound that makes them some of the most-used voicings, from contemporary rock and pop styles to traditional classical compositions. Add these to your Bar Chords Template we started back on the Third Floor, when we constructed the Traditional Triad Family: 3-note voicings.

Good Work!

Foundations Forms, another important stage of construction, is now complete. You should have fifteen sheets of 4-part 7th and 6th chords in all inversions, from major 7th quality to diminished major 7th quality. That is a lot of chords! Some you will use every day. Some may be for a specialized job, the fingerings of which you may never use again.

Because they hurt and should have been put in the dumpster!!

Yes, Chester. But as we have just seen with the A°Maj7 close voicing, as we create other chord qualities from these templates, some difficult, or impossible fingerings may become easier, so don't toss out anything yet!

And some of the sounds may tweak your fancy because of their uniqueness. Some of the inversions sound really intriguing and can be great catalysts for your creative work! Which is just one reason why this construction project is so much fun! Let's grab that elevator to the Fifth Floor. Onward, Chester!

CHAPTER 5: FIFTH FLOOR

5-PART CHORDS: ADDING ONE TENSION

Now, let's build upon our Foundations work and extend the 4-part chord forms we have just completed. These *ex-tensions*, more commonly called tensions, are the continuation of the degrees of the basic 7th chord or 6th chord. It is again the tertial system at work, building in thirds. Don't forget that simple triad down there, holding everything up! Let's add the first tension, the 9th degree. Remember that as we pile the thirds, we are creating another triad and another 4-part chord. That is why there are so many enharmonic look-alikes with assumed-root chord forms (**AR**) for the 4-part 7th and 6th chords.

Here are the chord tones of a CMaj7(9) chord in root/close position. Notice the E–7 chord created with the 3rd, 5th, 7th, and 9th degrees.

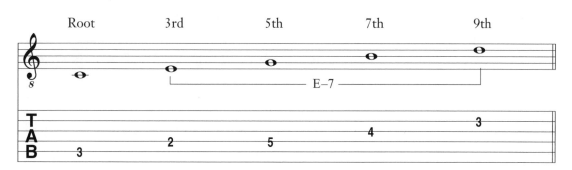

Fig. 5.1. CMaj7(9) Chord Tones

ABOUT *EXTENSIONS*

Tensions add interval color to a 4-part chord. They also add another possible note to help in voice leading a note of a chord into a next chord. In general, they add to our accompaniment resources. Tensions are *not* special effects. In fact, in certain idioms of music, they are a very common part of the harmonic vocabulary. Many standard-tune lead sheets will give a simple 4-part chord as a chord symbol, for example G7, and leave it up to the player to use tensions appropriate to the idiom and the melodic line being accompanied.

Wow, that's a lot of responsibility!

Some lead sheets have specific tensions written in the chord symbols. For example, G7($\flat$9, $\flat$13) may appear. Now, you *really* have responsibility! I actually prefer when simpler chord symbols are used, giving me more aesthetic choice.

In some instances, if you see a basic bare-bones G7 chord symbol, playing a bare-bones 4-part tensionless G7 chord may be the perfect choice. What you play is really up to your musical judgment, honed through experience.

Of course, you always have artistic license to do anything you wish with a chord. It depends on how "stylishly correct" you wish to be.

The following information here on the "Fifth Floor" is based on mainstream popular music language—status quo stuff. You can try more adventurous harmonic ideas that conflict with these basic ideas. That is what art is all about! The information here will give you a basic starting point and vocabulary.

Each basic 4-part chord quality is extended with its own series of tensions indigenous to it. For example, a major 7th chord quality can have a natural 9th as a tension but never a flat 9th or a sharp 9th. On the other hand, the dominant 7th chord quality is much more liberal-minded and has many more tension possibilities, depending on the chord's function in a chord progression. Dominant 7th chords can function as a tonic or restful sound, as in a blues progression. In this restful function, generally gentle natural tensions—natural 9th and 13th, for example—are used. But as this same dominant 7th chord begins to become more of a transitional, restless type of a chord, your choice of tension possibilities climbs.

Since "what tension to use?" with dominant 7th chords can be a very common question, I will try to explain. This is a very general look at use of tensions with dominant 7th chords.

First, some generally "consistent" dominant 7th tension situations. I put consistent in quotes since the only consistency in art and life is change. Any details expressed in this book are stylistic. They can be broken if the artist (you) desires.

Again, a dominant 7th chord can often be a tonic or I chord, as in a blues. In this situation, it generally takes on natural, bright tensions; 9 and 13.

What do you mean by natural or bright, Jon?

I use "bright" to mean a consonant sound and dark to mean a dark, dissonant quality. A tension degree such as natural 9 or natural 13 does not create "prime dissonance," such as minor seconds against a basic chord tone, the root, 3rd, or the 5th degree. Degrees such as ♭9, ♯9, or ♭13 do create prime dissonances, or dark tensions.

Dominant 7th chords can also often move *chromatically* downward to a major or a minor chord. Here is a chromatically moving dominant 7(9) chord in action.

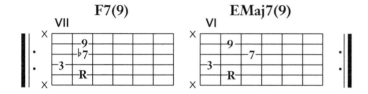

Fig. 5.2. F7(9) to EMaj7(9)

In this chromatic cadence situation, the dominant 7th chord again can take on natural tensions: natural 9th and/or natural 13th. They work nicely. By work, I simply mean stylistically, a la popular-music tendencies. Remember that learning about all these "status quords" will give you a great foundation to create revolutionary new ideas! Another good reason for our construction project.

Now for a can of worms.

Probably the most common use of a dominant 7th chord is as a V7 chord actively moving cycle V to a tonic or restful I chord. This situation has more variables.

Wait, first, just tell me what tensions I can use with dominant 7th chords.

Sure, Chester. May I introduce the "Bright/Dark Rap Chart" here, to hopefully clarify using tensions with dominant 7th chords.

THE BRIGHT/DARK CHART

A GENERAL TENSION GUIDE TO CYCLE-V MOVING DOMINANT 7TH CHORDS

To choose a tension, first look at the target chord that the dominant 7th chord is leading to.

If the target chord is a minor chord, with a dark chord quality, then tensions for the dominant 7th chord *generally* should be dark: ♭9,♯9, and/or ♭13. This prepares the transition for the dark, minor quality coming up. Using bright tensions going to minor is seldom done, since the transition from bright to dark isn't very uplifting now, is it?

On the other hand, the dominant 7th chord moving to a bright target chord, with a major quality, can use dark *and/or* bright tensions. Anything goes!

Of course, the final choice of tension(s) the accompanist uses must work with the tune's melody or with a solo that is being supported.

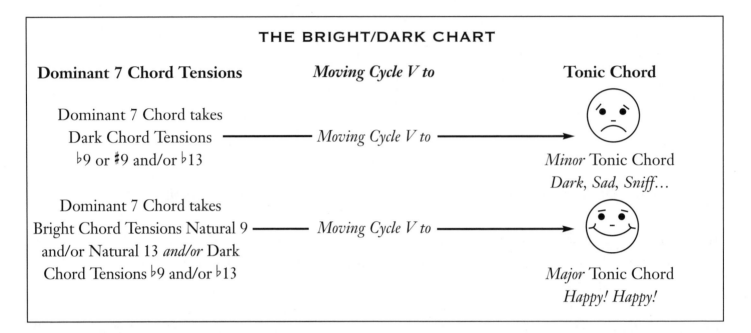

THE BRIGHT/DARK CHART

Dominant 7 Chord Tensions	*Moving Cycle V to*	**Tonic Chord**

Dominant 7 Chord takes
Dark Chord Tensions ———— *Moving Cycle V to* ————→
♭9 or ♯9 and/or ♭13

Minor Tonic Chord
Dark, Sad, Sniff…

Dominant 7 Chord takes
Bright Chord Tensions Natural 9 ——— *Moving Cycle V to* ———→
and/or Natural 13 *and/or* Dark
Chord Tensions ♭9 and/or ♭13

Major Tonic Chord
Happy! Happy!

Fig. 5.3. Bright/Dark Chart

Can you show this Bright/Dark Chart in action?

Sure, Chester.

Here is a dominant 7th chord, A7(♭9,♭13), moving to a minor tonic chord, a D-6. The dark tensions of the dominant 7th chord really set up the motion to the dark minor quality.

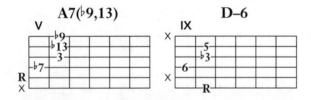

Fig. 5.4. A7(♭9,♭13) to D–6

Here is a dominant 7th chord, A7(♭9,13). The combination of dark and bright tension qualities on the dominant 7th chord has a nice contrast moving to the bright major tonic chord, the DMaj7, for which I used a bar chord.

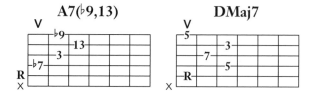

Fig. 5.5. A7(♭9,13) to DMaj7

Remember, this is a general look at tensions on dominant 7th chords moving in cycle V. I hope it helps a bit. There are many other examples of dominant 7th tension chords in action throughout the book.

Here on the Fifth Floor, certain degrees of the basic 4-part chords will be shifted or replaced to become tension degrees. The root may be shifted up to become the 9th degree (in tension language, 2nd degrees are called 9ths). The 5th degree may be shifted up to become the 13th degree (in tension language, 6th degrees are called 13ths). The 5th degree may also be moved down to become the 11th (in tension language, the 4th degree is called the 11th degree). As we have already seen, shifting notes around can create duplicities of chord shapes. These duplications can be beneficial. Use them to your advantage.

Let's grab those 4-part 7th chord Foundation Forms Templates you built in the last chapter, and put them to work!!

We'll start our tension building process with tension 9, the first extension to the 4-part 7th chord forms. We will follow the 9th chords with 11th and 13th chords. By adding the 9th degree, the 4-part chords now become 5-part chords.

Since our chording hand can only physically grab so many notes, we must be efficient. In fact, some of these 5-part chords may only have four notes in them! In general, to create 9th chords from the basic 4-part forms, *the 9th degree will replace the root.*

Now, finally….

ASSUMED-ROOT CHORD FORMS

If a root has been replaced by a 9th degree, it is called an assumed root (AR) chord. Sometimes this "missing root" can be physically added as a fifth voice. Of course, a bass player will help with the root note also.

That is, if they show up to the gig!

Right, Chester!

Since the 9th degree should sound like an extension or higher degree, it should not generally be placed too low in a chord form. With 4-part chords, where the root in the bass is on the guitar's low E and A strings, an option plan may be used.

OPTION-SHIFT PLAN FOR LOW ROOTS

Shift the 3rd degree down two frets to become the 9th (2nd degree), and then shift the 5th degree down three frets to the 3rd degree. See figure 5.6 with a major 7th chord.

The first quality we will add a 9th to will be the major 7th chord, to create major 7(9) chords. Several forms on the Major 7 Chord Template have the root in the bass on the low E, A, or D strings, perhaps too low to replace with the 9th degree, so let's try the option-shift plan mentioned above. Here are a few major 7 forms with low roots and then the forms with the option-shift plan in effect. This shift plan will add some nice tension chords to your dictionary.

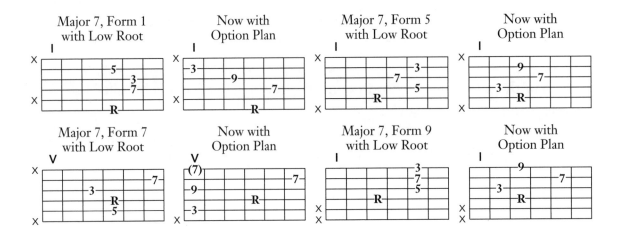

Fig. 5.6. Option-Shift Plan for Tension 9

Also, for creative reasons, you may wish to keep the 5th degree in its original position. This produces an interesting voicing that has a 9th but no 3rd degree.

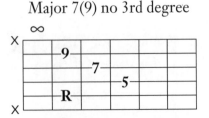

Fig. 5.7. Major 7(9) No Third Degree

THE 9TH CHORDS

MAJOR 7(9)

Chord Degrees: Root, Major 3rd, Perfect 5th, Major 7th, Natural 9th

Common Symbols: CMaj7(9) or C △ 7(9) or C $\frac{7}{}$(9)

Grab a blank sheet and create a Major 7(9) Template. Simply copy the Major 7th Template but shift the root degree up two frets to become the natural 9th degree. Remember, the option-shift plan from the above example is to be used when the form has the root in the bottom on the low E and A strings.

When an option plan is used, label the voicing accordingly.

Here is what the first major 7(9) should look like. Look at the first voicing on the Major 7 Template. Since the root is in the bass, on the low E string, we'll use the option-shift plan. Try it on the rest of the major 7th forms with root in the bottom on the low strings, as shown above. For the most part, the higher the 9th degree, the better.

First Major 7(9) Template Form
Option Plan

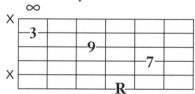

Fig. 5.8. First Major 7(9) Template Form

These major 7(9) forms are "pretty" chords and sound cool just by themselves. They are usually used as resting points in progressions.

Say Jon, can I show you two major 7(9) forms in action?

Let's hear them, Chester.

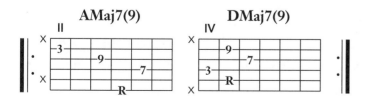

Fig. 5.9. AMaj7(9) to DMaj7(9)

Nice voicings and nice delivery, Chester. I like that Brazilian groove you are using. Obrigado!

Obie who?

Obrigado means "thanks" in Portuguese, the language of Brazil.

Cool!

Note 1

To create these major 7(9) voicings, if you physically can, add the root as a *fifth* voice on an available unused string. We had replaced the root with the 9th, but it's great if you can put it back in there. Go right ahead! Add this to the voicing as an option. Put it in parentheses.

This is voicing 2 on the Major 7(9) Template.

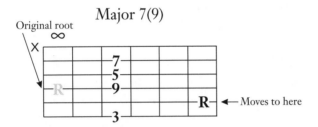

Fig. 5.10. Voicing 2 on the Major 7(9) Template

Occasionally, the 5th degree can be moved to become the root. See the example below of voicing 3 from the Major 7(9) Template. I'll leave the rest up to you to find.

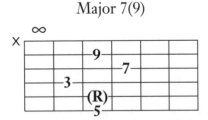

Fig. 5.11. Voicing 3 on the Major 7(9) Template

Note 2

Try open strings, when they are physically and tonally possible. They can fill in a root real nice!! Wow! I am finding *new* stuff, even after forty years of holding this box! Some of those funny looking forms towards the bottom of the page are starting to look like great candidates for some open-string voicings.

We'll find lots more in the "Open Strings" chapter (chapter 8) of the dictionary-building process.

So I just finished my Major 7(9) Template. You will find some interesting voicings.

I found that last row of close-position forms to be impossible, Jon!

Chester, don't even try to play some of those fingerings. As I mentioned before, be patient. As other qualities are explored, possibilities will appear.

MAJOR 6(9)

Chord Degrees: Root, Major 3rd, Perfect 5th, Major 6th, Natural 9th

Common Symbols: CMaj6(9) or CMaj(6,9)

For the Major 6(9) Template, copy the Major 7(9) Template we just built and shift the 7th degree down two frets to become the natural 6th degree. Here is what the first voicing should look like.

First Major 6(9) Template Form

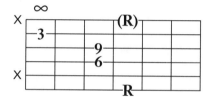

Fig. 5.12. First Major 6(9) Template Form

The major 6(9) chord is another pretty sound and works nicely along with major 7th and major 7(9) qualities, and also as a substitute. The major 6(9) is also a fairly indigenous sound in the beautiful music of Brazil. Here is a simple vamp for study that incorporates both the major 6(9) chord and the minor 6(9) chord colors. Play this vamp with a bossa nova or samba groove, or any groove that feels good to you.

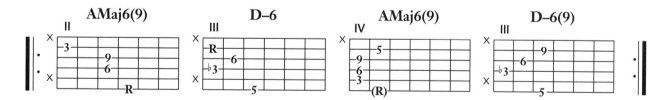

Fig. 5.13. Major 6(9) in Action

Those major 6(9) chords sound really mellow, like a well-administered neck rub.

Chester, I think *you* need a break!

But we're on a roll and I like these tension voicings!

Okay, Chester. Next stop: dominant 7(9).

DOMINANT 7(9)

Chord Degrees: Root, Major 3rd, Perfect 5th, Flat 7th, Natural 9th

Common Symbols: C7(9) or C9

For the Dominant 7(9) Template, copy the Major 7(9) Template, but shift the major 7th down one fret to the flat 7th.

Here is what the first voicing should look like.

First Dominant 7(9) Template Form

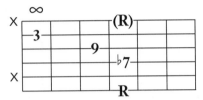

Fig. 5.14. First Dominant 7(9) Template Form

Again, as an option, or if moving the 5th degree down is not possible, simply keep the 5th degree in its original position. This produces an interesting voicing that has a 9th but no 3rd degree.

Dominant 7(9) No 3rd Degree

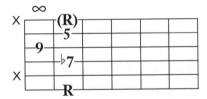

Fig. 5.15. Dominant 7(9) No 3rd

As you can hear, the dominant 7(9) chord has a bright quality, especially when heard next to this next chord quality.

DOMINANT 7(♭9)

Chord Degrees: Root, Major 3rd, Perfect 5th, Flat 7th, Flat 9th

Common Symbols: C7(♭9), C7(–9)

For the Dominant 7(♭9) Template, copy the Dominant 7(9) Template sheet, but shift the natural 9th degree down one fret to become the flat 9th degree. Here is what the first voicing should look like.

First Dominant 7(♭9) Template Form

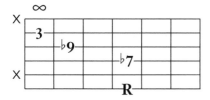

Fig. 5.16. First Dominant 7(♭9) Template Form

The dominant 7(♭9) is more intense—darker in quality than its dominant 7(9) colleague. It is a nice transitional chord when the lowered 9th degree moves chromatically downward in resolution, as in this simple example in G major.

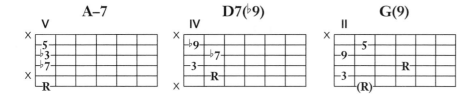

Fig. 5.17. Dominant 7(♭9) in Action

Say Jon, I saw a chord symbol "G7Alt." in one of my tune books. What's up with that?

The chord suffix "Alt." means "altered," which is requesting the altering of the 5th degree and/or the natural 9th degree up or down a half step. So what you meant is, "What's up, or down with that?"

What?!

DOMINANT 7(♯9)

Chord Degrees: Root, Major 3rd, Perfect 5th, Flat 7th, Sharp 9th

Common Symbols: C7(♯9), C7(+9)

For the Dominant 7(♯9) Template, copy the Dominant 7(9) Template sheet, but shift the natural 9th degree up one fret to become the sharp 9th degree. Here is what the first voicing should look like.

First Dominant 7(♯9) Template Form

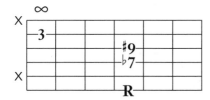

Fig. 5.18. First Dominant 7(♯9) Template Form

Ouch!!!

Yes, I know, Chester. Remember to try some of these stretch voicings higher up the fingerboard or drop out a note, like the root.

This first voicing has an intense dark quality, since there is a minor second between the 3rd and ♯9th degrees—the top two voices of the chord form. At first, I questioned its potential, until I tried it in a percussive Latin groove resolving to a minor chord.

Also, I once briefly thought about starting a Harmonotherapy scam in which I purport-edly would heal folks by playing chords "over them." I would use this Dominant 7(♯9) voicing to heal warts.

That chord sounds more like it would cause warts, Jon!

Yes, well, let me try playing this voicing in action for you.

I'll make things easier here by using an open A string for the root of the A7(♯9) chord and as the 5th degree of the D–6 chord. This repeated note is called an "ostinato." Effective. Play it as a montuno or as a *vamp*—a repeated rhythmic groove.

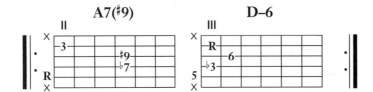

Fig. 5.19. First Dom7(♯9) Template Form in Action

Nice Brazilian stuff! I like that voicing now, after hearing it in action.

As they say in Portuguese, "Porque não?"

As I continued, I found some new favorites along with one of Jimi's favorites, chord 3 of this, the Dominant 7(♯9) Template.

One of Jimi's Favorites

Fig. 5.20. One of Jimi's Favorites

MINOR 7(9)

Chord Degrees: Root, Minor 3rd, Perfect 5th, Flat 7th, Natural 9th

Common Symbols: C–7(9), CMin7(9), Cmin7(9)

For the Minor 7(9) Template, simply copy the Dominant 7(9) Template sheet, but shift the major 3rd down one fret to become the minor 3rd degree.

Here is what the first voicing should look like.

First Minor 7(9) Template Form

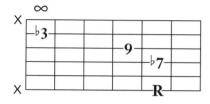

Fig. 5.21. First Minor 7(9) Template Form

That one was a bit tough to grab.

It is friendlier up the fingerboard, as figure 5.22 illustrates. Here is a nice descending passage using this voicing.

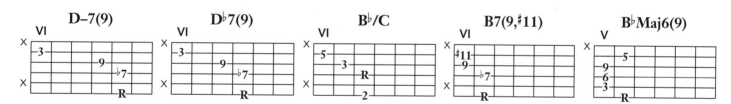

Fig. 5.22. Descending Chords

I like how the top voice of the chords stays the same in that example, Jon.

When there is movement (in this case downward) in some voices against an ostinato or repeated note, it is called "oblique motion." A nice musical effect.

MINOR MAJOR 7(9)

Chord Degrees: Root, Minor 3rd, Perfect 5th, Major 7th, Natural 9th

Common Symbols: C–Maj7(9), C–△7(9), C–7̶

For the Minor-Major 7(9) Template, simply copy the Minor 7(9) Template sheet but shift the flat 7th degree up one fret to become the major 7th degree.

Here is what the first voicing should look like. These first option-plan voicings of the tension 9 templates are the toughest ones to grab, as you have noticed. They do have personality, though. This is a beautiful, mysterious chord quality. My guitar hero Tony Mottola loved this quality and used it to great effect on an old boob-tube show called *Danger!* in which the guitar was the only instrument used for the soundtrack.

Very cool! I put this chord quality into action in figure 5.25, along with the minor 6(9) chord coming right up.

First Minor Major 7(9) Template Form

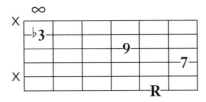

Fig. 5.23. First Minor Major 7(9) Template Form

MINOR 6(9)

Chord Degrees: Root, Minor 3rd, Perfect 5th, Major 6th, Natural 9th

Common Symbols: C–6(9), Cmin6(9), Cmin(6,9)

For the Minor 6(9) Template, simply copy the Minor 7(9) Template sheet, but shift the flat 7th degree down one fret to become the 6th degree. Move tension 9 to the top E string, if needed. Here is what the first voicing should look like.

First Minor 6(9) Template Form

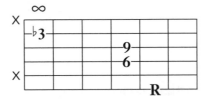

Fig. 5.24. First Minor 6(9) Template Form

We mentioned montunos or repeated harmonic grooves used in Latin music in figure 5.19. Here, I put the minor-major 7(9) chord quality to work moving to a minor 7(9) chord moving to a minor 6(9) chord. Alternate that low open E string and the 5th degree. You can make this slow or get it cookin'.

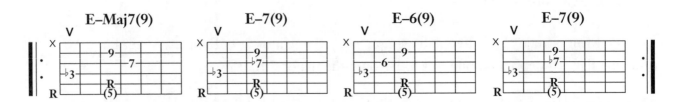

Fig. 5.25. E–Maj7(9) to E–7(9) to E–6(9) Montuno

The first chord above is from your tune "Poiple" from your *Dedications: Faces and Places* CD with Bill Frisell.

Bill who?! Another plug, Chester. Say…who are you, my agent?

Just send me 10 percent!

DOMINANT 7SUS4(9)

Chord Degrees: Root, Perfect 4th, Perfect 5th, Flat 7th, Natural 9th

Common Symbol: C7sus4(9)

For the Dominant 7sus4(9) Template, simply copy the Dominant 7(9) Template sheet, but shift the 3rd degree up one fret to become the suspended 4th degree. Move tension 9 to the top E string, if needed. Here is what the first voicing should look like.

First Dominant 7sus4(9) Template Form

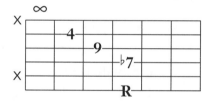

Fig. 5.26. First Dominant 7sus4(9) Template Form

Here is an example of the dominant 7sus4(9) chord moving to a dominant 7(♭9) chord, then on to a final resolution.

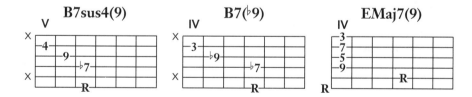

Fig. 5.27. First Dominant 7sus4(9) in Action

Now let's try some other tension colors.

First, we will add a 6th degree as a tension to a major 7th chord. In dominant 7th chords, the 6th degree is called tension 13, as we will soon see and build, but often the 6th degree relative to a major 7th chord is simply called a 6th even though it adds a nice tension quality. Also, many folks use the terminology "13" in their chord-symbol writing.

Crazy music lingo.

MAJOR 7(6)

Chord Degrees: Root, Major 3rd, Perfect 5th, Major 6th(13), Major 7th

Common Symbols: CMaj7(6) or a C△7(6) or C⅂(6) or CMaj7(13)

This is a pretty chord, the major 7(6) quality, a nice gentle chord that adds a simple tension color to a major 7th chord, a 6th degree. We can use two different shift techniques here. First, simply copy the Major 7 Template, but shift the 5th degree up two frets to become the 6th degree. Here is what the first voicing should look like.

First Major 7(6) Template Form

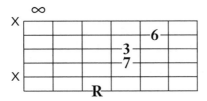

Fig. 5.28. First Maj7(6) Template Form

For 5th degrees that are too low, try this option plan. Again, use the Major 7 Template, but shift the 7th degree down two frets to become the 6th degree and shift the root down one fret to become the 7th. This technique will find some more possibilities if the first technique produces a difficult fingering. Here is the technique used with voicing 3 from the Major 7 Template.

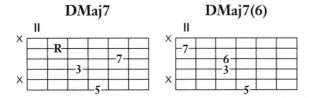

Fig. 5.29. Maj7 Voicing 3 to Maj7(6) with Option Plan

Try this shift plan with any of the major 7 forms.

I started to find so many nice voicings with the option plan that I did two templates: one for each shift technique. I found some sweet possibilities, and some crazy grips, also!

What do you mean by "grips," Jon?

The term "grip" is slang that refers to a guitar chord fingering or voicing.

Well, I am really having fun finding new grips, but how can I remember all this option plan stuff?

Good question, Chester! That's what we're here for! The option plans are temporary techniques to help us find other possible voicings. Once you find an interesting voicing, use it in action. It will become part of your vocabulary.

Remember that musical ideas that are now part of your instinctive abilities were at one point fairly intellectual. In fact, to prove this, try "The Incredible Time-Machine Study" in the "Break Room" (chapter 12). It will take you back in time.

Sounds a little scary to me!

Go ahead, Chester.

I'll start working with the next tension level, tension 11, the sixth part of a chord in our tertial system.

THE 11TH CHORDS

In this chapter, we are exploring 1-tension color possibilities. Since we only have so many fingers on our chording hand, we replace some degrees with tension degrees, as we did with tension 9 replacing the root. Here with tension 11(the 4th degree), the 5th degree *or* the 3rd degree will be shifted to become the tension 11(4).

MAJOR 7(♯11)

Chord Degrees: Root, Major 3rd, Flat 5th or Sharp 11th, Major 7th

Common Symbols: CMaj7(♯11)

The Major 7(♯11) Template forms will be the same as the Major 7♭5 Template we already created in Foundation Forms. Simply copy the Major 7♭5 Template sheet, but change the heading to Major 7(♯11) and write the flat 5th degree as the sharp 11th degree. Here is what the first voicing should look like.

First Major 7(♯11) Template Form

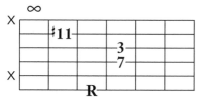

Fig. 5.30. First Maj7(♯11) Template Form

If the ♯11 appears too low, you will find that with the major 7(♯11) an option plan would be to copy the Major 7 Template but shift the 3rd degree *up* two frets. The 3rd degree is now not in the voicing, creating a more subtle quality. The 5th degree and the sharp 11th have a nice richness that makes the absence of the 3rd degree pretty acceptable. In fact, some of them are downright pretty! Here is Major 7 Template voicing 9 shifted using this plan. This plan creates some nice options. Include both possibilities in your dictionary if they work for you.

Major 7 Voicing 9 to Maj7(♯11) with Option Plan

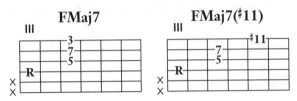

Fig. 5.31. Maj7 Voicing 9 to Maj7(♯11)

In my fake book, I see a lot of tunes with Maj7(♯11) chords.

You're right, Chester. It is a popular sound. Try using it as an inspiration for an original tune! Joe Henderson's tune "Inner Urge" has seven Maj7(♯11) chords in it!

DOMINANT 7(♯11)

Chord Degrees: Root, Major 3rd, Perfect 5th, Flat 7th, and Sharp 11th

Common Symbol: C7(♯11)

For the Dominant 7(♯11) Template, simply copy the Major 7(♯11) Template we just completed, but change the heading to Dominant 7(♯11), and move the major 7th degree down one fret to flat 7. Here is what the first voicing should look like.

First Dominant 7(♯11) Template Form

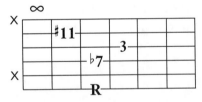

Fig. 5.32. First Dominant 7(♯11) Template Form

As with the Maj7(♯11) option plan, try shifting the 3rd degree up to become the sharp 11th degree.

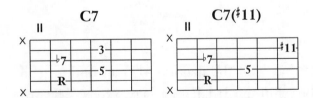

Fig. 5.33. Dominant 7(♯11) Option Plan

This chord is often used as a final chord in a blues or as a final chord for many tunes. It's got that "cool" sound. Cool is of course relative. In Mr. B's hands, every chord is cool.

MINOR 7(11)

Chord Degrees: Root, Minor 3rd, Perfect 5th, Flat 7th, Natural 11th

Common Symbols: C–7(11)

For the Minor 7(11) Template, simply copy the Minor 7 Template but shift the 5th degree *down* two frets to become the natural 11th degree.

Here is what the first voicing should look like.

First Minor 7(11) Template Form

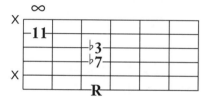

Fig. 5.34. First Minor 7(11) Template Form

That sure looks a lot like a dominant 7sus4 chord!

Right Chester, it's one of those enharmonic look-alikes.

An option plan for Minor 7(11) would be to copy the Minor 7 Template, but shift the flat 3rd degree up two frets to become the 11th degree.

Here is the Minor 7 voicing 9 becoming a Minor 7(11) using this option plan. I again created two separate sheets, one for each plan.

Minor 7 Voicing 9 to Minor 7(11) with Option Plan

Fig. 5.35. Minor 7 Voicing 9 to Minor 7(11) with Option Plan

Tension 11 on a minor 7 chord is a very user-friendly tension and can be placed in any register, even in the bass.

How can this be possible with a tension? I thought tensions had to be higher in a chord's register?

In general, that is true, Chester. In the case of tension 11 on a minor 7th chord, the tension can work low in the chord, because it doesn't create unwanted dissonances and does not change the basic function of the minor 7th chord.

MINOR 7♭5(11)

Chord Degrees: Root, Minor 3rd, Flat 5th, Flat 7th, Natural 11th

Common Symbol: C–7♭5(11)

For the Minor 7♭5(11) Template, the flatted 5th degree is so important to the chord quality that we cannot move it to the 11 unless we can also include the flat 5 on another string. So we will replace the flat 3rd degree with tension 11. Simply copy the Minor 7♭5 Template, but shift the 3rd degree up two frets to become the natural 11th degree.

Here is the first voicing—a stretcher, intense with the 11 and flat 5 degrees buzzing as minor 2nd neighbors. First, try it higher up the fretboard as a B–7♭5(11).

First Minor 7♭5(11) Template Form

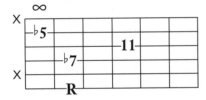

Fig. 5.36. First Minor 7♭5(11) Template Form

I tried it as a B–7♭5(11) and continued with this cadence possibility in A minor. The E7 is technically incomplete with no flat 7th, but I liked the minor second on the B–7♭5 so much that I kept it around. Dramatico! No? We will explore more "incomplete" chord possibilities a bit later. Sometimes, the incomplete voicing sounds perfectly complete.

What?

Sorry for the confusing language, Chester.

I also apologize for these stretches on this example. I just like the bite of those minor seconds!

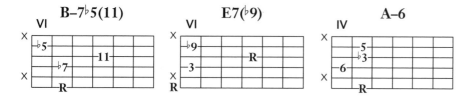

Fig. 5.37. Minor 7♭5(11) in Action

Now, let's try some 13th chords. The 13th degree is the seventh part of our Tertial System of chords.

THE 13TH CHORDS

DOMINANT 7(13)

Chord Degrees: Root, Major 3rd, Perfect 5th, Flat 7th, Natural 13th

Common Symbol: C7(13)

For the Dominant 7(13) Template, simply copy the Dominant 7 Template but shift the 5th degree up two frets to become the natural 13th degree. Here is what the first voicing should look like.

First Dominant 7(13) Template Form

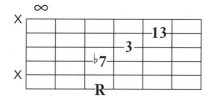

Fig. 5.38. First Dominant 7(13) Template Form

Option Plan: If the 5th degree is too low to become a 13th degree or if a voicing is hard to grab, try this option plan. Shift the flat 7th degree down one fret to become the 13th degree, then move the root down two frets to the flat 7th degree. Here is an example using chord 7 from the Dominant 7 Template.

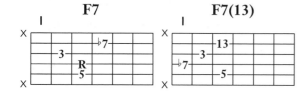

Fig. 5.39. Dom7(13) Option Plan

The option plan really helped me to find some nice possibilities for Dominant 7(13) chords. In fact....

Hey, Jon!! Check out this hot dominant 7(13) chord I found using the option plan! I added a 9th degree, since a string was available.

Fig. 5.40. Chester's Hot Find

Nice grip, Chester! A bit of a grab, but it sounds very cool.

I tried Chester's find up the neck a bit, as an E7(9,13) using the open E string as a nice low root. Let's not forget to include this voicing in our template construction in the next chapter, our explorations with two tensions.

"A blues a day will keep the doctor away...."

—Mr. B.

At first, I thought Mr. B had his own Harmonotherapy scam operation going when he first said this to me.

Not Mr. B!!!

Right, Chester. One of my mentors. It was playing these rich dominant 7th chords that reminded me of Mr. B's quote. In fact, a dominant 7(13) chord, like the dominant 7(9), is commonly used for a tonic or restful dominant 7th starting chord as in a blues. This next example, "A Blues a Day," begins with a B♭7(9) voicing followed by a darker B♭7(♭13) voicing to help the transition to the second bar, the IV chord E♭7(9). Remember that tensions are *not* special effects. They simply give us more tones to work with to create a desired melodic motion through a chord progression. Also used here are dominant 7th chords with two tensions, again to simply achieve a desired melodic motion. Play this example in a sweet, slow groove to appreciate the tensions moving by. I finished up the study with a nice neat B♭7(9).

"A BLUES A DAY"

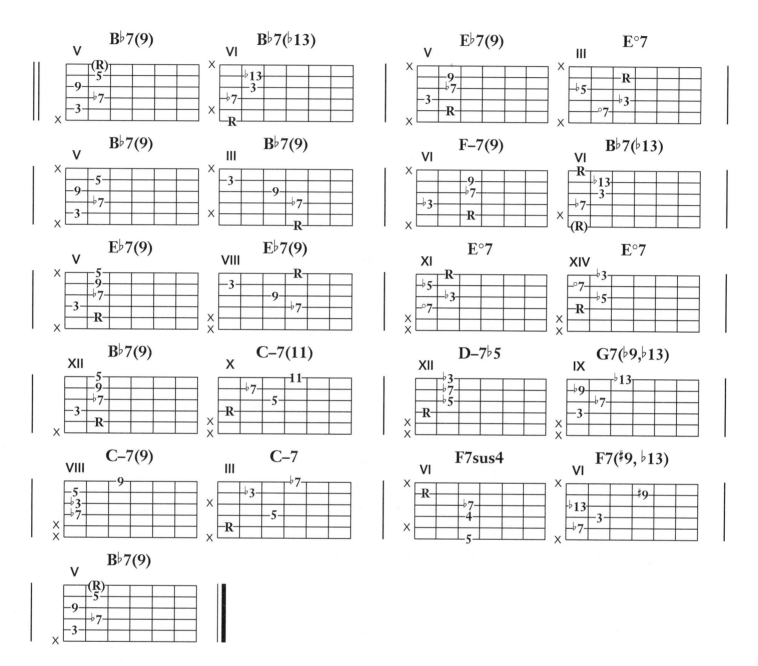

Fig. 5.41. A Blues a Day

That's cool, baby!

Why thanks, Chester. What's with the beret?

Playing "A Blues A Day" inspired me to wear it! It helped my delivery, man!

I think the Harmonotherapy benefits Mr. B referred to by prescribing "A Blues a Day" were its great therapeutic sound and playing value, and also its benefit as a wonderful harmonic study, rich with chord qualities and tension possibilities.

DOMINANT 7(♭13)

Chord Degrees: Root, Major 3rd, Perfect 5th, Flat 7th, Flat 13th

Common Symbol: C7(♭13)

It is challenging to find voicing possibilities for the dominant 7(♭13) chord. A flat ninth, a strong interval as you know, is created if the 5th degree is below the flat 13th degree. Also, some forms are just *too hard to grab*. The voicings with the flat 9th are pretty intense, but may, if grabbable, work in a musical situation. Perhaps they are not effective as a dominant 7(♭13) but as an effective chord with some bite to it.

For the Dominant 7(♭13) Template, simply copy the Dominant 7(13) Template we just completed, but *shift the natural 13th degree to the flat 13th degree*. Here is what the first voicing should look like.

First Dominant 7(♭13) Template Form

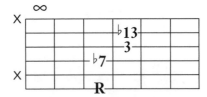

Fig. 5.42. First Dominant 7(♭13) Template Form

As we saw in the "A Blues a Day" example, this chord can be used as a V7 chord going to a minor chord. The flat 13th degree is, in fact, the same note as the minor 3rd degree of the minor chord it is resolving to. I am using a nice open-string C–(9) chord here in figure 5.43. You may remember it from chapter 2. It has that nice ♭9 richness in it.

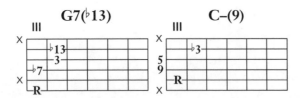

Fig. 5.43. Dominant 7(♭13) in Action

DOMINANT 7SUS4(13)

Chord Degrees: Root, Perfect 4th, Perfect 5th, Flat 7th, Natural 13th

Common Symbol: C7sus4(13)

For the dominant 7sus4(13) Template, simply copy the Dominant 7(13) Template, but shift the 3rd degree up one fret to become the sus 4th degree. Here is what the first voicing should look like.

First Dominant 7sus4(13) Template Form

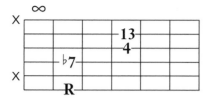

Fig. 5.44. First Dominant 7sus4(13) Template Form

You're afraid to add a tension to a diminished 7th chord, ain't ya, Jon?

Why no, Chester.

In fact, we have already used a tension tone on a diminished 7th chord in the last chapter when we built the diminished major 7th chord forms. With diminished 7th chords, any degree a whole step above a basic chord tone is a tension degree. The 9th degree is a whole step above the root. The 11th degree is a whole step above the flat 3rd, the flat 13th is a whole step above the flat 5th degree, and the tension 7 is the tension tone above the diminished 7th degree.

Wow, that's a mouthful!

DIMINISHED 7TH CHORDS AND THEIR TENSIONS

To find these tension forms, take your Diminished 7 Template sheet, and copy the forms, *raising one of the basic degrees a whole step (two frets) when possible*. As you can see, there are many duplicate forms on each row of the basic template. Do the four possibilities in each row, labeling the tensions accordingly. Label the heading Diminished 7 Tension Forms. Label each form with the appropriate tension.

Figure 5.45 is what my first row of diminished 7th chords with 1-tension forms looks like.

Remember, a diminished 7th chord often functions as a dominant 7($\flat$9) chord, so adding a "tension" may produce an awkward sound relative to the active tonality. Generally, these "tensions" are played more as approach tones to create some activity with a diminished chord. The original degree position is in regular text two frets below the tension, which is in bold type along with the rest of the diminished 7 with 1-tension voicings.

First Row of Dim7 Template with 1-Tension

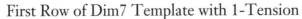

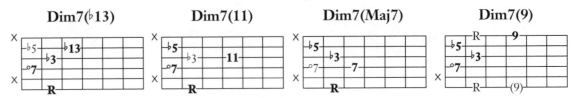

Fig. 5.45. First Row of Diminished 7 Template with 1-Tension Forms

Those diminished chords have me depressed now!

I know how you feel, Chester.

1-TENSION BAR CHORDS

Let's finish up this floor with some 1-tension bar chords. They may cheer you up a bit.

1-Tension Bar Chords

Fig. 5.46 1-Tension Bar Chords

I feel better already. Those minor 7(11) voicings are pretty mellow.

Good, Chester.

ADDING TWO OR MORE TENSIONS

TENSIONS LOVE COMPANY AND SO WILL OUR HANDS!

Yep, tensions love company. The second tension gives us more melodic potential when voicing through a chord progression. It can create a nice sound support for the first tension, and it also occasionally gives our chording hand a break. Less stretching.

Here is an example of how this can work.

Play figure 6.1, a dominant 7(9) form moving to the form with a 13th added; the 5th moves up two frets to the 6th or 13th. Hear how the addition of the 13th creates solidity in the chord sound. Your hand may ergonomically like this form better also.

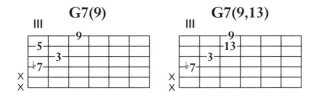

Fig. 6.1. Dominant 7(9) Moving to Dominant 7(9,13)

Say Jon, in my tune fake books, I could barely find any chord symbols with two tensions. In fact, I didn't find too many 1-tension situations. Do we really have to learn these guys?

Yes, it is true. In general, lead sheets and fake books consist generally of simple 4-part 7th chord chord symbols with an occasional tension thrown in. The usage of tension colors is totally up to the player interpreting the chord symbols.

The Bright/Dark Chart back on the Fifth Floor really helped me, in that regard.

Good, Chester.

In music specifically arranged or composed for film and theater productions, recording sessions, and celebrity concerts, chord symbols with one or more tensions are *very* common, since specific tensions are used by the arranger or composer in their writing for the rest of the orchestra.

So, yes, we are learning to work with these tension chord symbols in order to give us more harmonic resources for our improvised accompaniments, *and* to help us address and comfortably play any chord symbol we might encounter.

THE TWO-AND-MORE-TENSION FORMS

MAJOR 7(9,♯11)

Chord Degrees: Root, Major 3rd, Perfect 5th, Major 7th, Natural 9th, Sharp 11th

Common Symbols: Maj7(9,♯11) or △7(9,♯11) or 7̄(9,♯11)

To create the Major 7(9,♯11) Template, simply copy the Major 7(♯11) Template but shift the root degree up two frets to become the natural 9th degree. If a resulting 9th degree is too low (as in the first voicing), if possible, move the 9th to a higher string. The first major 7(9,♯11) voicing should look like this.

First Major 7(9,♯11) Template Form

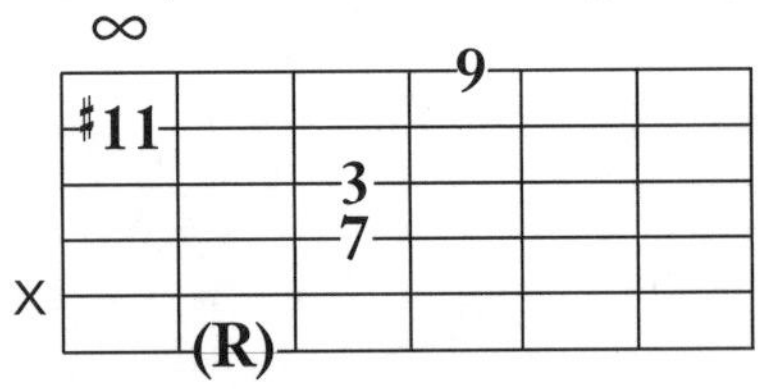

Fig. 6.2. First Major 7(9,♯11) Template Form

Also, a ♯11 tension will sound better if shifted higher in the voicing. Here is voicing 3 with the sharp 11th shifted to the high E string.

Voicing 3 with ♯11 Shifted to High E String

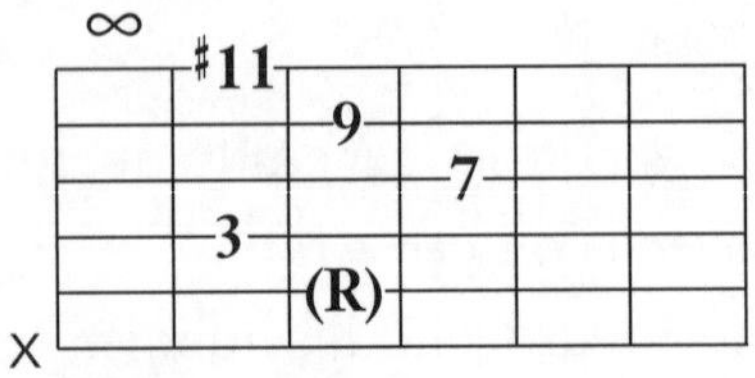

Fig. 6.3. Voicing 3 with ♯11 Shifted to High E String

Try similar octave shifts of low tensions throughout these tension explorations. Don't worry if a tension must remain low in a voicing. In a higher register, this same voicing will work fine. Also try moving a 3rd degree down two frets to become 9 or shift a 9th to an available string. Grab it, if possible. A nice example can be found in the Major 7(9,6) Template coming up.

MAJOR 7(9,6)

Chord Degrees: Root, Major 3rd, Perfect 5th, Major 7th, Natural 9th,
                      Major 6th

Common Symbols: CMaj 7(9,6), C 7((9,6), C △ (9,6)

To create the Major 7(9,6) Template, simply copy the Major 7(9) Template but shift the 5th degree, when available, up two frets to become the natural 6th degree.

The first major 7(9) voicing had no 5th, so here is voicing 2 from the Major 7(9) Template shifted to a major 7(9,6).

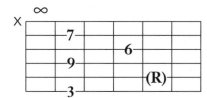

Fig. 6.4. Voicing 2 Major 7(9,6) Template Form

Say Jon, since the 6th degree was available on the high E string, I created this Maj7(9,6) voicing from the first Maj7(9) voicing.

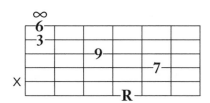

Fig. 6.5. First Major 7(9,6) Template Form

Good work, Chester. Using an available string is a great idea.

MAJOR 6(9,♯11)

Chord Degrees: Root, Major 3rd, Perfect 5th, Major 6th, Major 7th,
                      Natural 9th, Sharp 11th

Common Symbol: C Maj6(9,♯11)

To create the Major 6(9,♯11) Template, simply copy the Major 6(9) Template but shift the 5th degree, when available, down one fret to become the sharp 11th degree.

The first major 6(9) voicing had no 5th degree, so here is the third voicing from the template shifted to a major 6(9,♯11). Notice that I moved the sharp 11th degree to the high E string from its position on the low E string. If you wish, try moving a 3rd degree up two frets to ♯11 to find more possibilities.

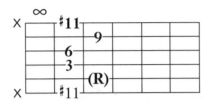

Fig. 6.6. Major 6(9,♯11) Template Form

I look forward to working with the dominant 7th chords with two tensions. So many possibilities! I'm afraid we'll run out of fingers.

No worries, Chester. In fact, this is a good time to introduce the Guide Tone Templates to you.

THE GUIDE TONES TEMPLATES

Before we dive into the complex world of tension possibilities with the dominant 7th chord quality, may I share an interesting chord search option: Guide Tones (G.T.) Templates. These G.T. Templates help me see the fingerboard from "another angle." In building some of the 2-tension dominant 7th chord templates, I became frustrated with the replacement game—13 for 5, etc.—since I was running out of fingers and coming up with some strange and painful results because of very low tensions and no possible option plans.

Since the guide tones—the 3rd and 7th degrees of the 4-part 7th chords—are general essentials to a chord's character, I decided to work with them, as a simple foundation to help support my two-and-more-tension explorations.

G.T. TEMPLATES

BASED ON A C ROOT TONAL CENTER

Here are three G.T. Templates: Major 7, Dominant 7, and Minor 7. Using C natural as the root, I set the guide tones (3rd and 7th) for each chord quality in **bold white type** and in circles, and other degrees (including tensions) in plain type.

MAJOR 7 GUIDE TONES TEMPLATE

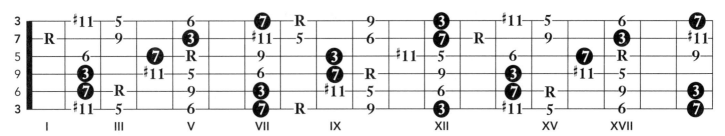

DOMINANT 7 GUIDE TONES TEMPLATE

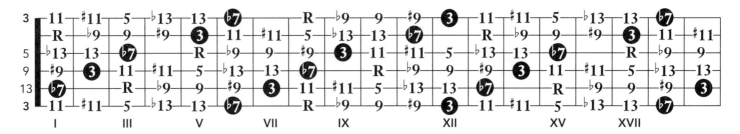

MINOR 7 GUIDE TONES TEMPLATE

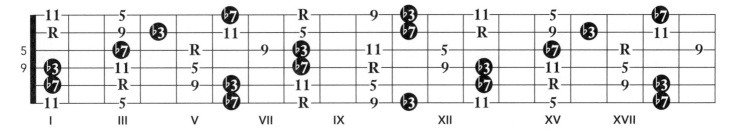

Fig. 6.7 Guide Tones Templates

How do these templates work? That's a lot of numbers!

As you glance at a G.T. Template, choose a pair of guide tones to work from: a 3rd and a 7th. Then look for tension possibilities on the other available strings. Try some of the voicings that magically appear. Start with the major 7 quality G.T. Template. Remember, try to keep guide tones lower in register than tensions. There are some nice exceptions, some of which I list below. You may find some forms we already explored earlier in this chapter, but you will also find some new forms.

Here are a few that I found. Since I didn't have a bass player around to provide me a root for these "root-less" harmonic characters, I put them over open string roots to hear the tension qualities better. In a band situation with a bass note provided, they sound fine. Watch those stretches. Don't forget to do your yoga in the "Break Room," chapter 12.

Major 7 with Two-Tension Forms from the Major 7 Guide Tones Template

AMaj7(6,♯11)   **EMaj7(6,9)**   **AMaj7(9,♯11)**

AMaj7(9,6)   **AMaj7(9,♯11)**   **EMaj7(9,♯11)**

Fig. 6.8. Major 7 with Two-Tension Forms from G.T. Template

Generally, place tensions higher in register. As you can hear in figure 6.8, you will also find interesting harmonic possibilities with tensions lower. Be careful of creating muddiness due to lower register intervals. Use your own discretion. Possibility is a subjective issue, especially in the arts. And we sure are curious artists!

Let's continue with the Minor 7(9,11) Template. We'll try first our "shift plan" technique, and then we'll search on the Minor 7 G.T. Template for tension 9 and 11 possibilities.

MINOR 7(9,11)

Chord Degrees: Root, Minor 3rd, Perfect 5th, Flat 7th, Natural 9th, Natural 11th

Common Symbol: C–7(9,11)

For the Minor 7(9,11) Template, simply copy the Minor 7(9) Template but shift the 5th degree, when available, *down* two frets to become the 11th degree.

Remember that tension 11 is a user-friendly tension and can appear fairly low in register, so more possibilities open up for us.

Say Jon, the first voicing on my Minor 7(9) Template doesn't have a 5th degree to move!

Voicing 1 did not have a 5th degree, Chester, since we used the option plan to create that voicing. Here is my first possibility. It is from voicing 2 of the Minor 7(9) Template. If needed, move the ♭3 degree up two frets to 11(4).

First Minor 7(9,11) Template Form

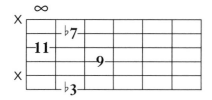

Fig. 6.9 First Minor 7(9,11) Template Form

Here are two pretty voicings I found using the Minor 7 G.T. Template. The first one is a serious stretch. I put them both over open strings as roots, to hear the tension qualities better. It is fun using the G.T. Templates. Possibilities appeared that I might never have found, since the templates give a "panoramic view" of the fingerboard. In fact, this is the first time I ever played these voicings, and after more than forty years of searching!

Minor 7(9,11) Voicings from Guide Tones Template

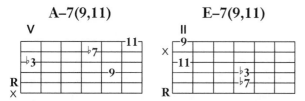

Fig. 6.10. Minor 7(9,11) from G.T. Template

Cool voicings. I am going to work with the G.T. Templates tonight. See you in the morning, Jon.

Okay, good afternoon, Chester. I may work through to the morning.

Let's continue now with the rich array of dominant 7th chords with 2-tension possibilities. We will explore a combination of plans to produce voicings, using our shifting degrees plan and working from the G.T. Templates.

As with many chords, when heard by themselves, some of these dominant 7th voicings may sound puzzling. As I have been doing with other chord qualities, I will use these 2-tension dominant 7th's in action for you to try. I will sketch in some examples in a bit. First let's dive into this series of 2-tension dominant 7th chords.

On all of these chord templates, I am keeping the guide tones intact, as part of each dominant 7th voicing. This is not always necessary, and at the end of the chapter, we will explore this possibility with 3-tension structures.

DOMINANT 7(9,13)

Chord Degrees: Root, Major 3rd, Perfect 5th, Flat 7th, Natural 9th, Natural 13th

Common Symbol: C7(9,13)

For the Dominant 7(9,13) Template, copy the Dominant 7(13) Template but *shift the root up two frets* to become the natural 9th degree. Move tension 9 to a higher string, if needed. Figure 6.11 shows what the first voicing should look like.

This chord quality with natural (bright) tensions works well on restful tonic chords, as we heard in "A Blues a Day," back on the Fifth Floor.

First Dominant 7(9,13) Template Form

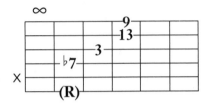

Fig. 6.11. First Dominant 7(9,13) Template Form

That search with the shift plan was somewhat productive, but there were some strange results, as I expected. That is why I felt that the G.T. Templates would help.

Here is a dominant 7(9,13) I found from the G.T. Template.

Dominant 7(9,13) from G.T. Template

Fig. 6.12. Dominant 7(9,13) from G.T. Template

Next will be the dominant 7(9,♭13). For each of these upcoming dominant 7th chords with altered or dark tensions, I will show them in action with a possible resolution to a tonic chord, which reveals the powerful chromatic, cadential motion of these tensions as they move to rest.

DOMINANT 7(9,♭13)

Chord Degrees: Root, Major 3rd, Perfect 5th, Flat 7th, Natural 9th, Flat 13th

Common Symbol: C7(9,♭13)

For the Dominant 7(9,♭13) Template, simply copy the previous Dominant 7(9,13) Template but shift the 13th degree down one fret to become the flat 13th degree. Figure 6.13 shows what the first voicing should look like. I illustrate it moving to a restful tonic chord.

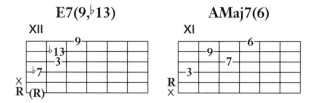

Fig. 6.13. First Dominant 7(9,♭13) Template Form in Action

And here is a dominant 7(9,♭13) grip I grabbed from the G.T. Template. I found the form pretty quickly.

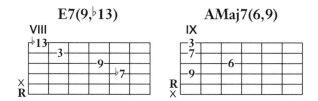

Fig. 6.14. Dominant 7(9,♭13) from G.T. Template in Action

DOMINANT 7(♭9,13)

Chord Degrees: Root, Major 3rd, Perfect 5th, Flat 7th, Flat 9th, Natural 13th

Common Symbols: C7(♭9,13)

For the Dominant 7(♭9,13) Template, copy the Dominant 7(9,13) Template but shift the natural 9th degree down one fret to become the flat 9th degree. Here is what the first voicing should look like in action.

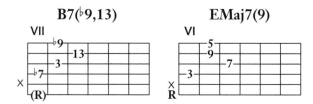

Fig. 6.15. First Dominant 7(♭9,13) Template Form in Action

This dominant 7(♭9,13) is a relative of the previous G.T. form, the dominant 7(9,♭13), as you can see. Why not? It works!

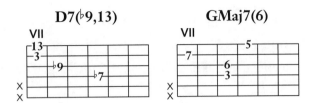

Fig. 6.16. Dominant 7(♭9,13) from G.T. Template in Action

DOMINANT 7(♯9,13)

Chord Degrees: Root, Major 3rd, Perfect 5th, Flat 7th, Sharp 9th, Natural 13th

Common Symbol: C7(♯9,13)

For the Dominant 7(♯9,13) Template, copy the Dominant 7(9,13) Template but shift the natural 9th degree up one fret to become the sharp 9th degree. Here is what the first voicing should look like.

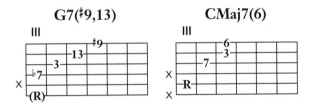

Fig. 6.17. First Dominant 7(♯9,13) Template Form in Action

I like the bite of this next dominant 7(♯9,13). The minor second between the flat 7th and 13th degrees helps, as well as the major seventh between the major 3rd degree and the sharp 9th! I resolved it to a major 7th chord with no 3rd degree. It works nicely. The G.T. Template at work. I bet Chester found some nice chord possibilities last night with the G.T. templates.

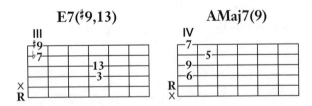

Fig. 6.18. Dominant 7(♯9,13) from G.T. Template in Action

DOMINANT 7(♭9,♭13)

Chord Degrees: Root, Major 3rd, Perfect 5th, Flat 7th, Flat 9th, Flat 13th

Common Symbol: C7(♭9,♭13)

For the Dominant 7(♭9,♭13) Template, copy the Dominant 7(♭9,13) Template but shift the natural 13th degree down one fret to become the flat 13th degree. Here is what the first voicing should look like, shown in action moving to a minor 6(9). Smooth stuff.

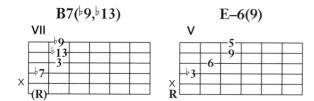

Fig. 6.19. First Dominant 7(♭9,♭13) Template Form in Action

This is one of the dominant 7(♭9,♭13) voicings I found from the G.T. Template. It is a bit pallid with the 3rd so low, but its uniqueness has piqued my interest.

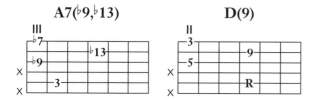

Fig. 6.20. Dominant 7(♭9,♭13) from G.T. Template in Action

DOMINANT 7(♯9,♭13)

Chord Degrees: Root, Major 3rd, Perfect 5th, Flat 7th, Sharp 9th, Flat 13th

Common Symbol: C7(♯9,♭13)

For the Dominant 7(♯9,♭13) Template, simply copy the Dominant 7(9,♭13) Template, but shift the 9th degree up one fret to become the sharp 9th degree. Here is what the first voicing should look like.

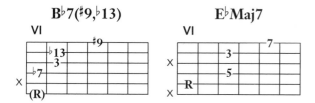

Fig. 6.21. First Dominant 7(♯9,♭13) Template Form in Action

And here is a possibility from the G.T. Template.

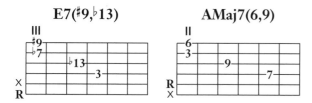

Fig. 6.22. Dominant 7(♯9,♭13) from G.T. Template in Action

Now for the dominant 7(9,♯11).

DOMINANT 7(9,♯11)

Chord Degrees: Root, Major 3rd, Perfect 5th, Flat 7th, Natural 9th, Sharp 11th

Common Symbol: C7(9,♯11)

For the Dominant 7(9,♯11) Template, simply copy the Dominant 7(♯11) Template but shift the root degree up two frets to become the 9th degree. Here is what the first voicing should look like. Don't forget to try moving a 3rd degree down two frets to the 9th degree, if needed.

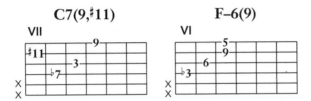

Fig. 6.23. First Dominant 7(9,♯11) Template Form in Action

I had to search the G.T. chart a bit, but found this interesting dominant 7(9,♯11) voicing. In this cadence, I have an E7(9,♯11) voiced in an exotic manner moving to an AMaj7♯5, another exotic sound for a contemporary touch. I'm sorry Chester is missing this. It's not like him to be late. One of my favorite aspects of chord searching is finding new unique voicings that take me somewhere special, perhaps to a seed for a new composition.

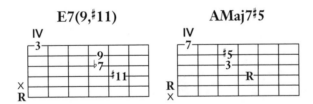

Fig. 6.24. Dominant 7(9,♯11) from G.T. Template in Action

Ah, it's morning! Chester is a bit late today.

DOMINANT 7(♭9,♯11)

Chord Degrees: Root, Major 3rd, Perfect 5th, Flat 7th, Flat 9th, Sharp 11th

Common Symbol: C7(♭9,♯11)

For the Dominant 7(♭9,♯11) Template, simply copy the Dominant 7(9,♯11) Template we just completed but shift the 9th degree *down* one fret to become the flat 9th degree. Here is what the first voicing should look like. Remember that the degrees in parentheses on the template are optional. The thumb of your chording hand can sometimes grab a note on the low E string. In fact, the great guitarist Tal Farlow had such enormous hands that his thumb was always helping out with his great chords.

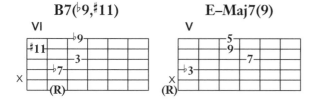

Fig. 6.25. First Dominant 7(♭9,♯11) Template Form in Action

Here is a G.T. Template find, simply a shifting of the natural 9th down to the flat 9th from the dominant 7(9,♯11). Remember that as you explore new finds, at first a sound may be perplexing, but with time it becomes part of your harmonic language. This new G.T. find for a dominant 7(♭9,♯11) is a bit strange for me, but here it is in action anyway.

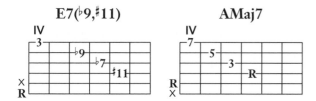

Fig. 6.26. Dominant 7(♭9,♯11) from G.T. Template in Action

Chester is still not here yet. I hope he's not gett...

Hi Jon. What'd I miss??? Sorry I'm late.

Good morning, Chester.

I got a good start on the dominant 7th 2-tension voicings with the added help of the G.T. Templates. Check them out. I'm just starting on this Dominant 7(♯9,♯11) Template.

DOMINANT 7(♯9,♯11)

Chord Degrees: Root, Major 3rd, Perfect 5th, Flat 7th, Sharp 9th, Sharp 11th

Common Symbol: C7(♯9,♯11)

For the Dominant 7(♯9,♯11) Template, again grab the Dominant 7(9,♯11) Template. Copy it but shift the 9th degree up one fret to become the sharp 9th degree. Here is what the first voicing should look like. It is quite a stretch.

First Dominant 7(♯9,♯11) Template Form

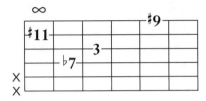

Fig. 6.27. First Dominant 7(♯9,♯11) Template Form

Chester, here is a form I found from the G.T. Template that is also a stretch but not quite as tough. Remember, try them out up higher on the fretboard.

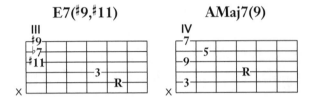

Fig. 6.28. Dominant 7(♯9,♯11) from G.T. Template in Action

I liked working with the G.T. Templates last night, Jon. Can I show you this sequence I found?

Sure, Chester.

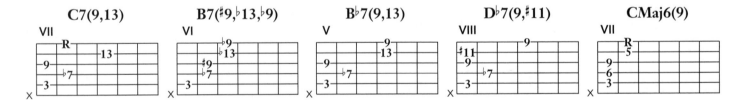

Fig. 6.29. Chester's Tritone Dominant 7 Explorations

Nice voicings, Chester, and a great example of how tensions simply give us more melodic possibilities for our harmonic vocabulary. I also like the way you started with your pretty dominant 7th discovery.

"Say Jon, that example I found was pretty cool ...ahhh ...did ...you ...ever find that one?"

Can't say I have... There are sooo many...

Yes!!!

Don't get bigheaded on me now, Chester.

Now, permit me to share a simple cadence in which the two tensions of the dominant 7th chord create two melodic lines that move in contrary motion as they resolve into the tonic chord. I first give a standard notation example to more clearly illustrate the contrary motion of the tensions, the top two voices of the E dominant 7th chords.

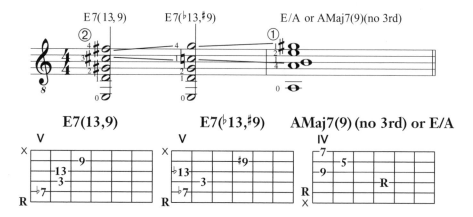

Fig. 6.30 Cadence with Two Tensions in Contrary Motion

Show off!

For the last two dominant 7th qualities, dominant 7(♯11,13) and dominant 7(♯11,♭13), I decided to use only the Dominant 7 G.T. Template to find structures, since the ♯11 and 13 are basically shifts from the 5th degree, and our previous templates were not very productive. So, here are some voicings for each of these.

DOMINANT 7(♯11,13)

Chord Degrees: Root, Major 3rd, Perfect 5th, Flat 7th, Sharp 11th, Natural 13th

Common Symbol: C7(♯11,13)

Dominant 7(♯11,13) Forms from G.T. Template

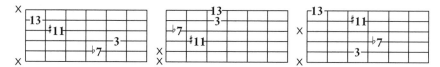

Fig. 6. 31. Dominant 7(♯11,13) Forms from G.T. Template

DOMINANT 7(♯11,♭13)

Chord Degrees: Root, Major 3rd, Perfect 5th, Flat 7th, Sharp 11th, Flat 13th

Common Symbol: C7(♯11,♭13)

Dominant 7(♯11,♭13) Forms from G.T. Template

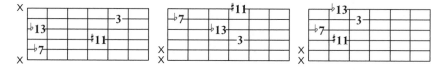

Fig. 6.32. Dominant 7(♯11,♭13) Forms from G.T. Template

Continue to explore the Guide Tone Templates for 2- and 3-tension possibilities. Remember that if you have the luxury of someone providing the bass and guide tones, then that really opens up some possibilities. In fact, here are some 3-tension voicings I gleaned from the G.T. Templates. Some have only one guide tone. By themselves, they may sound rather plain, and in fact, look exactly like some basic 4-part forms we found earlier in construction. I have provided an open string as a root when possible.

Some 3-Tension Possibilities from the G.T. Template

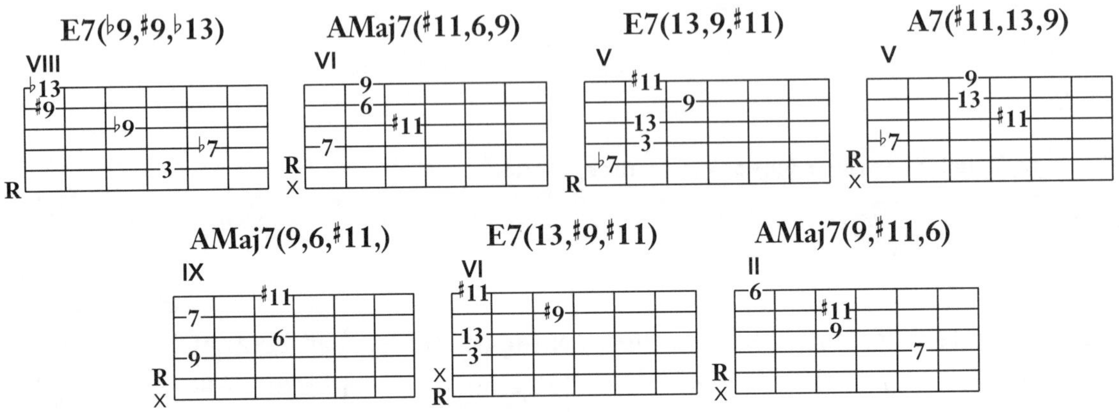

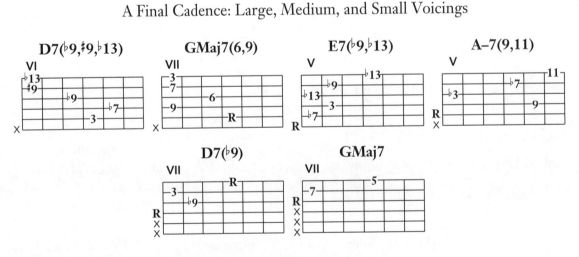

Fig. 6.33. Some 3-Tension Possibilities from the G.T. Template

A most important reason to build a varied harmonic vocabulary is so we can produce a range of sizes and textures harmonically in our playing and composing. In this final cadence of this chapter, I start with larger chord forms and end with small. I like the smaller guys. They are sweet. And simple. My favorites. Those big guys are just too darned hard to play!

A Final Cadence: Large, Medium, and Small Voicings

Fig. 6.34. Final Cadence: Large, Medium, and Small Voicings

TRIADS OVER BASS NOTES

In today's pop-music culture, slash chords—triads over bass notes—are common elements in chord progressions, from Sting to Scofield. The first time I saw a slash chord symbol, it scared me half to death! It may have just been a now docile-looking A/B chord—a simple A major triad sitting on top of a B natural bass note—but at the time, that chord symbol sure looked strange! Chord symbols like C7($\flat$9,$\flat$13) or F°(Maj7) were old hat to me, but just seeing that slash symbol for the first time visually twisted me around. In the "4-Part Chords" chapter, we referred to the term "slash chords" in describing enharmonic "look-alikes." As we saw, many of the 4-part 7th-chord qualities we found can also be looked at as various triads over bass notes, since that is exactly what they are. A root position CMaj7 chord is also an E–/C chord!

Some slash chords are simply <u>inversions of basic 4-part 7th chords</u>. C/B$\flat$ is simply the third inversion of a C7 chord. For our purposes, the term "slash chord" will pertain to any traditional triad over any bass note. Some folks delineate this population with terms like hybrid chords, upper structure triads, etc. We'll use the term "slash chords."

Here on the seventh floor of construction, we will build all the possibilities of triads over bass notes, as well as play some in action. Remember that the diagonal slash (/) symbol simply represents the word "over."

As we have seen, in the traditional Western European triad-based harmonic system, harmonies are essentially piled in thirds, creating traditional triads, and then piling on more triads as "extensions" on top of these. As we add another third, a B natural (the 7th) on top of a C major triad, another triad (E minor) is formed with the 3rd, 5th, and 7th degrees. Adding the next third, the 9th, creates a G major triad out of the 5th, 7th, and 9th degrees, and so forth.

Here are the chord tones and possible tensions of a CMaj7 chord. I have bracketed the triads that are formed in the structure.

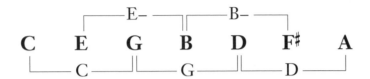

Fig. 7.1. Triads from C Major 7 with Tensions

THE SLASH CHORD TEMPLATES

To create a slash chord, we need room below the triad for the bass note, which is why the 3-part close triads found on the higher string sets are the best candidates for slash chords.

Since major triads are most often used for building slash chords, let's start with those. Grab a fresh template sheet, and label it Major Slash Chords. Take the Major Triad Template we built. Since we need room below a triad for the bass note, we will use the triads found on the top four strings, leaving our low E, A, and D strings for the bass note. The close triads we will build from are the six forms in the upper-right area of your Major Triad Template, page 1. Take the first close Major Triad form, which is on string set ② ③ ④. It is template 3 of your Major Triad Template.

Play the triad anywhere you wish along the string set. Now, add the closest note possible on an unused *lower* string below the major triad form.

Figure 7.2 is the first one I found. Label this first slash chord of the template sheet as I have, in this case, as a major triad over its 6th degree or Maj/6. This symbol is used only for our template reference. Depending on where you played it, the actual chord symbol would be written C/A or G/E or A♭/F, all major triads over their 6th degrees.

Maj/6

Fig. 7.2. First Major Triad for Slash-Chord Template Form

For the next slash chord form, move the bass note down a fret. Sketch it in, and label it Major/♭6(♯5). Continue in this manner.

Here is the first triad over all possible reachable bass notes. You will recognize some forms as enharmonic with other chord qualities. I have included all possibilities, including the triad over a doubled note like a 5th or a 3rd degree, which are common symbols used and produce nice 4-note traditional triad structures. Also sketch in an optional fingering with the degree in parentheses, as I have done below. Don't include impossible-to-grab grips!

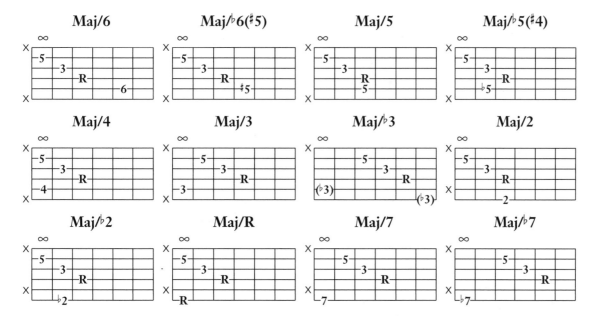

Fig. 7.3. First Major Triad through All Possibilities for Slash Chord Template Form

What a variety of colors! Some are quite tame and some are pretty wild!

With slash chords, we are exploring a range of tonal possibilities. The tame voicings are suggesting just one tonality or two "friendly" tonalities. Those wild guys are suggesting more than one tonality, and also that a richer relationship exists.

Continue with the rest of the close major triads in a similar manner. *Don't hurt yourself!* Here is the next major triad and its first two possibilties.

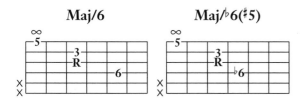

Fig. 7.4. First Two Slash-Chord Possibilities for Second Major Triad

Also work up templates for minor triad slash-chord possibilities.

If you wish to do the diminished and augmented triads, go right ahead. But the major and minor triads are most often used for slash-chord technique.

Why?

Chester, the major and minor triads exhibit a powerful independent tonal center, thanks to the perfect 5th degrees they both have. This helps separate the triads from the bass notes more effectively than the unstable diminished and augmented triads.

COUNTERPOINT WITH SLASH CHORDS

The exciting part of all this slash chord stuff is the contrapuntal possibilities! The slash visually creates a duality—two separate layers. With the chord symbol E/C, for example, it is very clear that two layers exist: an E major triad layer and a C bass note layer. Let's take advantage of this and try some fun contrapuntal possibilities. In fact, by taking a traditional-looking chord symbol and rewriting it as a slash chord, other visual and sound possibilities are stimulated.

Let's take a look at a good old CMaj7 chord, and rewrite it as an E–/C chord symbol.

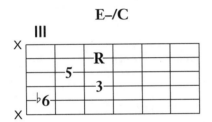

Fig. 7.5. E–/C

I know it looks strange, but now that we have two layers visually, let's take advantage and try some counterpoint thinking with the layers. First, let's try contrary motion. Move the E minor triad up to an F major triad and the C bass note down to a B♭, creating F/B♭. We now have:

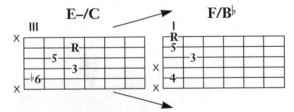

Fig. 7.6. Contrary Motion

Let's continue in contrary motion and see what evolves. This is fun. It feels like sketching or sculpting. What is nice is that we are moving the symbols with linear thinking.

Here is just one possible continuation of the progression. The top triad is moving up against the bottom bass note moving down.

$$\text{E–/C} \quad \text{F/B}\flat \quad \text{G/A} \quad \text{A/A}\flat \quad \text{B/G} \quad \text{C/F} \quad \text{D/E} \quad \text{F/D}\flat \quad \text{G/C}$$

We could have moved upward to any triad we wanted or downward to any bass note. The second chord could possibly be an intense F/B. I used the F/B$\flat$ for its mild intensity. So use your own aesthetic judgment when trying this stuff!

As with any harmonic progression, how you voice lead the progression will either make it or break it. Of course, delivering the progression musically is an integral part to the musical success of this or any other technique.

Here is the above progression using just one of many voice-leading possibilities. Use any groove you wish. I tried it with a fusion groove, and it worked out well. You can move from one voicing as quickly or as slowly as you wish.

Contrary Motion with Slash Chords

Fig. 7.7. Contrary Motion with Slash Chords

Hey Jon, my hands are feeling tired. Should I try some of those yoga stretches back in the "Break Room" chapter?

Chester, do the yoga stretches before and after any playing session. When your hands feel tired, it is time to stop playing. Moderation is important for the health of our hands and arms.

Now let's try some slash chords moving in oblique motion. In oblique motion, one layer repeats while the other layer moves. Here, the repeating layer will be simply a repeating sequence of a C major triad moving to an F major triad, and the bass line will be a descending chromatic line. This example has a nice gospel feel to it.

Oblique Motion with Slash Chords

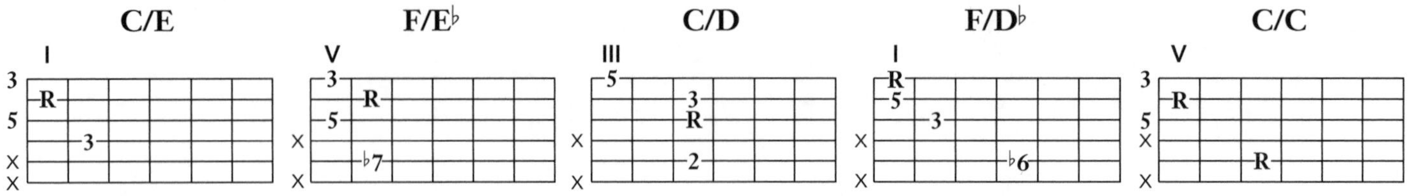

Fig. 7.8. Oblique Motion with Slash Chords

Another fun recipe of slash chord "cooking" is taking a standard harmonic progression, boiling down the chords to basic triads, and then putting those over a bass line. Here are the opening eight bars of "All The Things You Thought You Were but Wasn't" with its basic triads and a chromatically moving bass line. Remember that this is pretty modern thinking here, so use caution! I hope Jerome Kern isn't listening! I have placed the original chords above (in parentheses) for reference.

Again, this is one of many possibilities. This technique can sound as inside or outside as you aesthetically please.

"ALL THE THINGS YOU THOUGHT YOU WERE BUT WASN'T"
WITH SLASH CHORDS

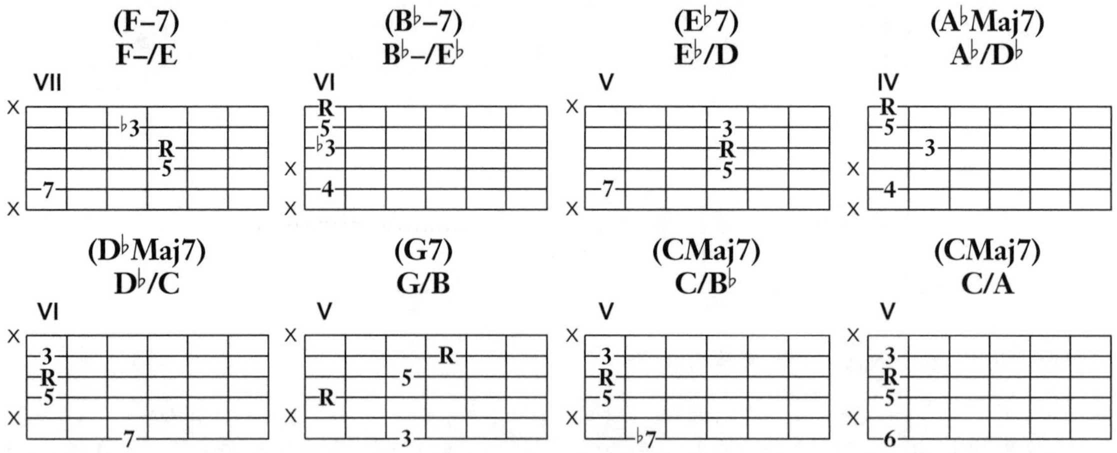

Fig. 7.9. "All the Things You Thought You Were but Wasn't" with Slash Chords

Here are some slash chord forms that give a contemporary touch to the classic chord progression "Rhythm Changes," which is based on the George Gershwin standard, "I've Got Rhythm."

RHYTHM CHANGES WITH SLASH CHORDS

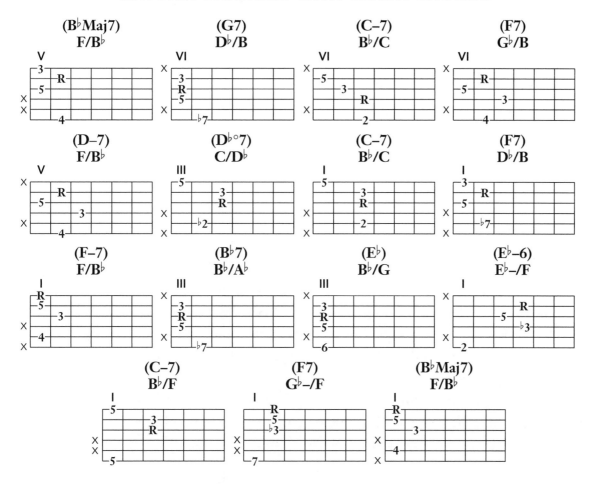

Fig. 7.9. Rhythm Changes with Slash Chords

How do I know which slash chord will work for a particular chord symbol?

Start with the possible triad extensions of a chord quality. For the first chord, B♭Maj7, I used an F triad over B♭, since the 5th, 7th, and 9th degrees of the B♭Maj7 chord create an F major triad. This technique is used twice for the C–7 chord, using a B♭ triad, which contains the ♭7, 9th, and 11th degrees of C–7. For the G7 chord, a D♭ triad is used which contains the ♭7, ♭9, and ♯11 degrees of G7. The D♭ triad is placed over the bass note B, the 3rd degree of G7. As your awareness of chord tones improves, you will be able to "see" and eventually hear slash chord possibilities more easily.

Looking at our "everyday" chord symbols from another angle, as with slash-chord possibilities, can really produce some interesting results. Now for another incredible world of chords, "Open-String Chord Forms." Elevator, Chester?

I think we need a walk, at this point!

OPEN-STRING CHORDS

VIII

Recently, a friend was impressed by all the cool chord voicings I was discovering as I was building my chord dictionary. He then mentioned, "I don't see any of those nice, simple, pretty, open-string forms indigenous to the folk and classical traditions." Here on the eighth floor, we will explore those nice, simple, pretty, open-string forms and also find many new and exciting chord forms in the fantastic world of open-string chords. An open-string chord form is simply a chord form in which one or more "unfingered strings," or open strings, are used in the chord. The open strings add a brilliant tone color to a chord and/or often enable us to play a voicing that would otherwise be impossible.

We have already met some open-string forms in action in some of the "in context" examples we have played, so some forms will be familiar to you, but most will not.

I will introduce three techniques here for exploring this exciting family of chords. Essentially, with an open-string form, the nut—the grooved piece of plastic or ivory that the strings ride over on their way to the tuning pegs—becomes an extra finger(s) to help us.

The easiest open-string form is the six open strings of our guitar!

Right, Chester. And, it has a name: E–7(11)!

E–7(11)

```
R
5
3
♭7
11
R
```

Fig. 8.1. The Simplest Open-String Form!

Now that was an easy grip! Our first open-string form. And it is moveable along the fingerboard! Many of the open-string forms we will find are not moveable. Like this form for AMaj7(9), playable at only one place on the fingerboard, which is special, I think. Like having a special marble that you have only one of. Like the world's most beautiful chord—that I will share with you shortly!

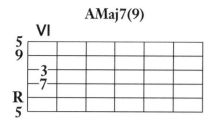

Fig. 8.2. Non-Moveable Open-String Form

OPEN-POSITION FORM TECHNIQUE

Now, let's get to work. The first technique for finding open-string chord forms will work with any of the chord forms we have already built in our construction process, which we can call "non-open string" chord forms. Simply grab a chord form, and move that form down until the nut takes over the job of some of your chord-hand fingers.

Here is a major 7th chord form in its totally fingered form and then as an open-string form, now specifically a GMaj7 form. The non-open string form is not new, but now with the open strings as part of the voicing, bright, new sound colors emerge.

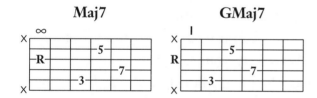

Fig. 8.3. Totally Fingered Form to Open-String Form

Here is another form, a major 7(9) form. It is presented in a totally fingered form and then with the nut helping out.

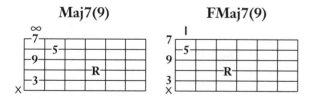

Fig. 8.4. Another Example

As you can see, this one technique alone will find many new open-string chord sounds. Let's start our first Open-String Forms Template working from our completed triad templates. Let's begin with the 5- and 6-note bar-chord forms.

Let's move the first major-triad bar chord down to open position and see what we find.

Major Triad Bar Chord   E

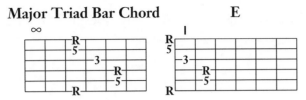

Fig. 8.5. Bar Chord to Open-String Form

I thought "open position" meant a chord that spanned more than an octave.

You're right, Chester! The term "open position" does refer to that type of chord. But it is also used to indicate the lowest playing position on the guitar—down by the nut and pegboard and using open strings. Double lingo, man!

Take one of your blank templates and title it Open-String Chord Forms. Start the Open-String Template working from the triad templates and the full- and half-bar forms we built way back on the "Third Floor" chapter.

Continue your open-string explorations with the other chord qualities we have constructed. Your dictionary will fatten quickly. Don't forget to find your own "in context" examples to help you incorporate these forms into your vocabulary.

ADDING OPEN-STRINGS TECHNIQUE

Here is another technique for finding open-string chord forms, with which I found one of my favorite chord voicings—my most-beautiful-chord-in-the-world form! This technique requires some theoretical know-how. Hopefully, your experience in the construction process has built up a harmonic understanding that will help with this technique.

As in the last technique, simply grab a chord form. Play it. First see if any "unused string(s)" can be opened up to add to the original. In this example, I found that for the first voicing, the open G string works nicely as the major 7th degree. And then I found that as I moved my hand down the fingerboard, the open G string became either a tension or basic chord-tone possibility, creating a nice "covey" of open-string major 7th chord forms.

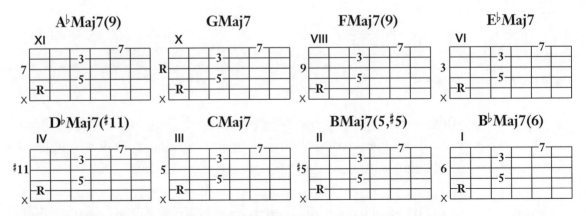

Fig. 8.6. A♭Maj7, a Favorite Voicing and a Covey of Open-String Maj7 Voicings

I like that first voicing, with the open G string. I played it *softly*, like droplets of water gently reaching for the pool below. . . .

What a delivery, Chester! Now you know why it is my favorite.

DROPPING FINGERS TO OPEN-STRINGS TECHNIQUE

Here is another possibility. Play any non-open string voicing you wish. Now if possible, lift a finger and play the open string that a fingered note was on. Observe the relationship of the open string. Does it work or not with the chord? Try using neighboring open strings also. Here are a handful of possibilities I found from this technique, just from using one fingering—my sentimental favorite, the close Maj7 chord fingering.

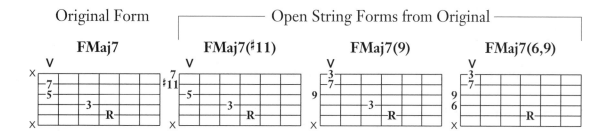

Fig. 8.7. FMaj7 with Open-String Variations

Another fascinating technique would be to take each open string and make it a particular degree of a chord, filling in the rest of the chord with available open and fingered notes. Here are a string of possibilities using the high open-E string as a 9th degree for various qualities.

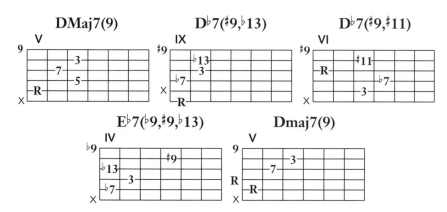

Fig. 8.8. A String of Possibilities

Jon, can I show you some open-string forms that I've found?

Of course, Chester. Go ahead.

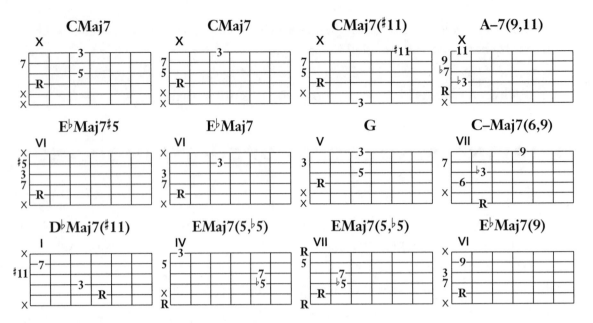

Fig. 8.9. A Few of Chester's Open-String Finds

That's a nice pile and variety of open-string voicings, Chester. Thanks. Don't forget to put those voicings in context to help you to remember them.

Here is a pretty open-string vamp I found. Meditative.

Hey, there's no place like Om!

"A MEDITATIVE CADENCE"

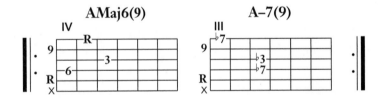

Fig. 8.10. A Meditative Cadence

The open-string chord form world is really like a can of worms. Organize this group of possibilities any way you can. Once you open yourself up to the possibilities, watch out!

As I mentioned earlier, your dictionary will never really reach completion. This is a good thing.

Say Jon, I finished *The Professor and the Madman*, and the ending was mind-boggling!!!

I know, Chester. You chord explorers should read this book!

Hey. guess what? We made it to the roof!!!

A LOOK AT THE PALETTE CHART

I've been waiting for these Palette Chart goodies since the Third Floor chapter!

I know, Chester, and thanks for your patience.

Since we finally made it up to the roof of our construction project, let's get a little fresh air. We began our construction with small, airy 2- and 3-note chord structures, then moved on to larger 4-, 5-, and 6-note structures. Now, let's take another look at some lighter 3-note forms again. On the third floor, we took a good look at the traditional triad family. Now Chester, as I promised, let's meet the other 3-note chord families. The 3-note chord structures can, of course, be found as integral parts of larger chord forms, as we have seen with the traditional triad family, but the most important benefit of a 3-note chord structure is its lightness and flexibility. Also, with fewer notes, the individual tone colors of a 3-note structure are heard more easily. The 3-note structures are also a cool contrast to use along with the larger chord forms.

As promised back on the third floor, here is a brief look at the Palette Chart, a system I created to visually display and organize the many possibilities of 3-note chord and melodic structures, or colors. I will give a basic overview of the Palette Chart to help our chord construction process. For an in-depth look at the Palette Chart, please refer to chapters 2 and 4 of *The Guitarist's Guide to Composing and Improvising*, a book in which I explore many harmonic and melodic possibilities inspired by the Palette Chart. This chapter is just a dip of the harmonic brush.

Corny!

Sorry. Here is the Palette Chart, Chester.

THE PALETTE CHART

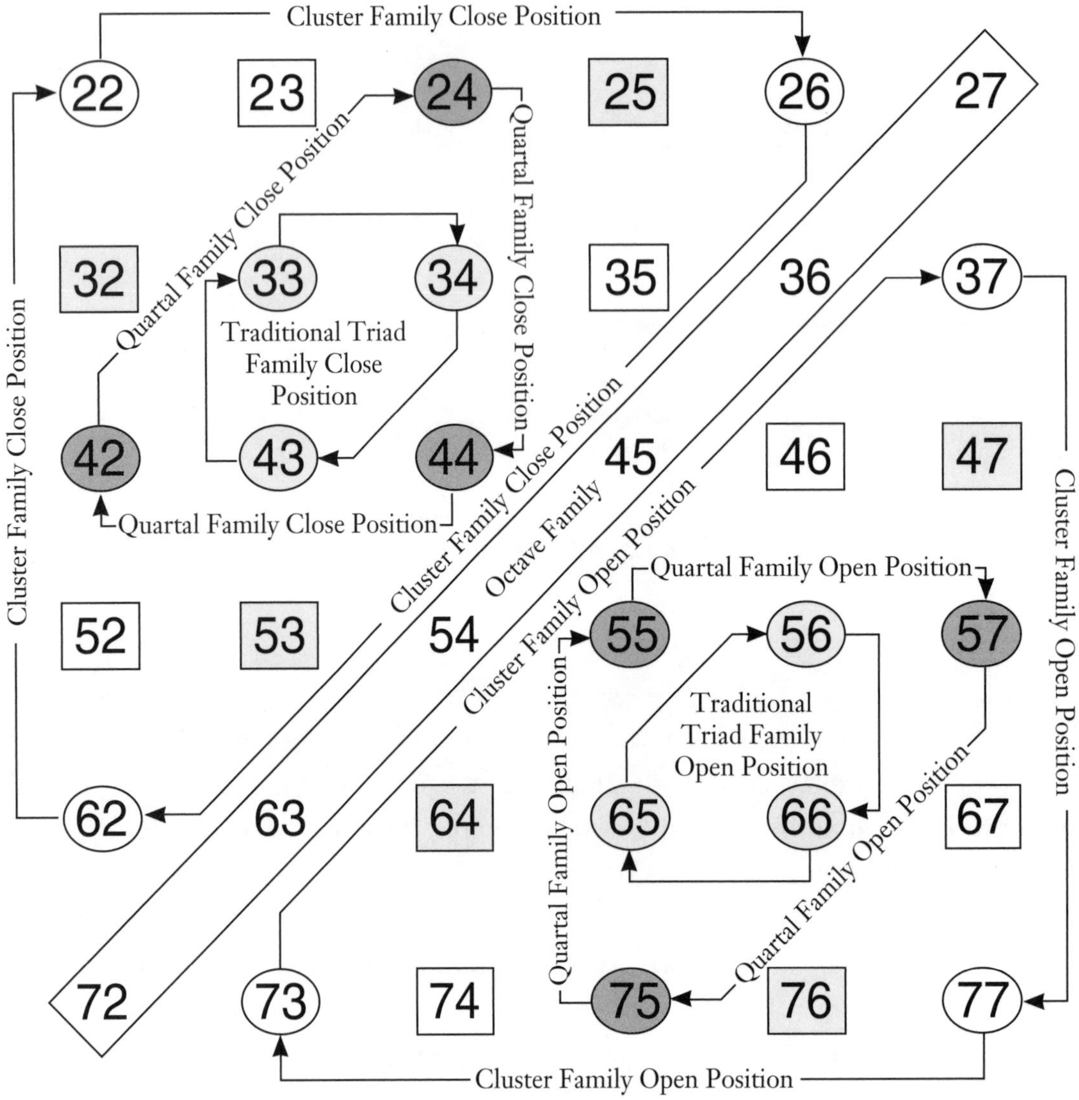

Cluster Family seeds are in white ellipses.

Traditional Triad Family seeds are in light grey ellipses.

Quartal Family seeds are in dark grey ellipses.

Seventh Chords No Fifth Family seeds are in white boxes.

Seventh Chords No Third Family seeds are in grey boxes.

Octave Family seeds are in a diagonal box.

Fig. 9.1. The Palette Chart

As you can see, that's a lot of numbers!

Wait a minute. Let me get my calculator.

It is pretty simple, Chester.

The groups of two numbers represent the intervals that make up 3-note structures. I call them "seeds." You will again see the value of "pure interval description" when discussing harmonic structures.

What do you mean by "seeds," Jon?

"Seeds" refers to the 3-note chords in the chart. Once you plant them in your imagination, incredible possibilities develop and grow from them.

Cool...

For our construction process of the Palette Chart families, find the blank fingerboard template in the "Tool Box" chapter. Copy about twenty of these, to get started. We will also refer to previous construction work to help us find these harmonic gems.

Here is a brief look at each family in the Palette Chart.

THE TRADITIONAL TRIAD FAMILY

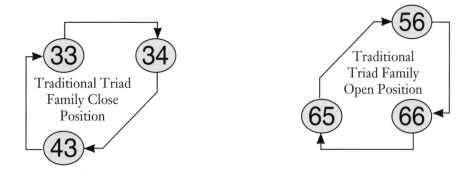

Fig. 9.2. The Traditional Triad Family

Find the Traditional Triad Family in close and open position on the Palette Chart. They are in light gray ovals and connected with arrows through the inversions. Coloring them in light blue will make it easier to see the link at a glance.

As we have been observing during construction and have already built, the traditional family of triads, or the "Tertial Family," is essentially built intervallically in thirds. The root-position, close-position form consists of a third piled on another third. This interval structure is indicated as ③③ on the Palette Chart.

First inversion is indicated as ③④ representing the intervals of a third and a fourth.

This family can be described easily with a chord symbol. Many of the 3-note structures on the Palette Chart cannot be described easily with a chord symbol. This is why the interval and family system helps to identify these 3-note colors.

THE QUARTAL TRIAD FAMILY

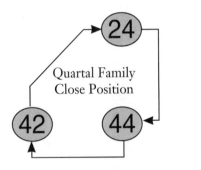
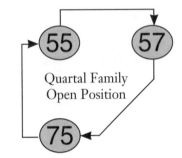

Fig. 9.3. The Quartal Triad Family

Find the Quartal Triad Family in close and open position on the Palette Chart. They are in dark gray ovals and connected with arrows through the inversions. Coloring these in yellow will make them easier to find.

The Quartal Triad Family is built basically on fourths in close position. As with any chord structures, other intervals are created as inversions, and open-position forms are created.

The Quartal Triad Family is a wonderful modern sound, but actually is one of the earliest of harmonic structures. Some of the open-position Quartal Triad Family Forms may remind you, again, of Gregorian Chant. In the "Modern Period," many musicians from Debussy to Bill Evans to Yngwie Malmsteen have worked with this family. And now us!

Grab a blank fingerboard template, and let's build the 44 seed. Since the scale is the basic building block for our tertial system, let's use it here with the other triad families. For a basic visual guide, let's use a C major scale as a foundation. Eventually, you should work these families through C melodic minor and C harmonic minor.

Yikes!!!

Here is the 44 triad moving diatonically in the key of C major along the top set of three strings. Continue and work out the rest of this family on the templates.

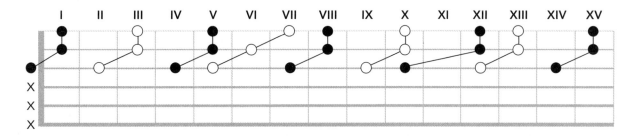

Fig. 9.4. 44 Seeds along the G, B, and High E Strings in C Major

THE CLUSTER TRIAD FAMILY

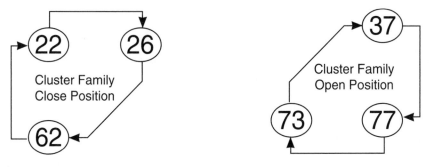

Fig. 9.5. The Cluster Triad Family

Find the Cluster Triad Family, close and open position, on the Palette Chart. They are in clear ovals and connected with arrows through the inversions. Color these in light purple for clarification.

Like clusters of grapes!

And I thought I was corny!

The Cluster Triad Family is essentially built in seconds in "close position." It expands, as all families do, through their inversions and open forms.

In fact the ㉒ seed is basically impossible to play without open strings! But its inversions and open forms are more user-friendly.

The rich color of this family is popular and can be heard from the Beatles to Zappa to Bill Frisell. Here is the ㉖ seed on the top string set. Explore the rest of this beautiful family.

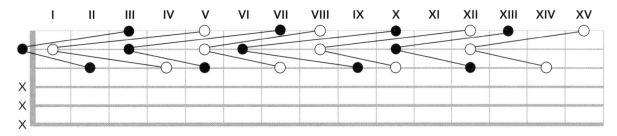

Fig. 9.6. 26 Seeds along the G, B, and High E Strings in C Major

These clusters sound really nice!

That's a nice fusion groove you are using, Chester. It works well with the cluster seeds.

THE 7TH CHORDS NO 5TH TRIAD FAMILY

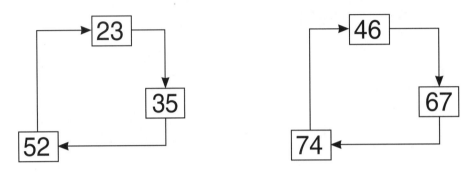

Fig. 9.7. The 7th Chords No 5th Triad Family

Find the 7th Chords No 5th Triad Family on the Palette Chart. They are in clear boxes. This family is simply the 4-part forms we created back on the fourth floor without the 5th degree. Choose your own color here. The essential 7th chord quality is maintained, but now with only three notes, they are lighter and again more flexible. They sound great along with larger chord forms and are also a nice foundation for walking bass-line technique. Another possible way to find the forms for this family is to refer to the 4-Part 7th Chord Templates and remove the 5th degrees. Or proceed with a fingerboard Template as we did with the Quartal and Cluster families.

Here are the 74 seeds along the fingerboard's low E, D, and G strings.

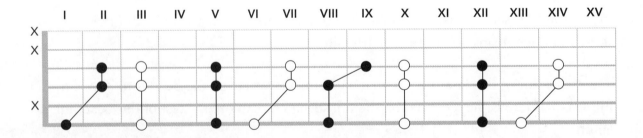

Fig. 9.8. 74 Seeds along the D, G, and Low E Strings

You're right about using the 74 seeds for harmonizing a bass line. They sound great with a Freddy Green—like quarter-note groove.

Nice sounds, Chester. Thanks to the beret?

THE 7TH CHORDS NO 3RD TRIAD FAMILY

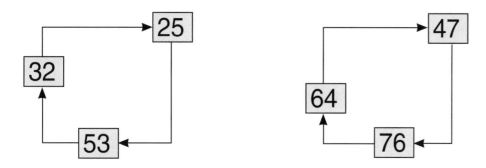

Fig. 9.9. The 7th Chords No 3rd Triad Family

Find the 7th Chords No 3rd Triad Family on the Palette Chart. They are in light gray boxes. This family is simply the 4-part forms we created back on the fourth floor, but now without their 3rd degrees. The essential 7th or 6th chord quality is subtler now, without the defining 3rd degree, but they also sound great along with larger chord forms. As we have already heard in some of the playing examples, they are a refreshing sound next to the more "obvious" chord structures. As with the 7th Chords No 5th Family, another possible way to find the forms for this family is to simply refer to the 4-Part 7th Chord Templates and remove the 3rd degrees. Or again, proceed with a fingerboard template, as I have done below.

Here is the 53 seed along the G, B, and high E strings.

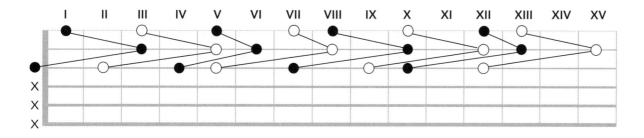

Fig. 9.10. 53 Seeds along the G, B, and High E Strings

THE OCTAVE TRIAD FAMILY

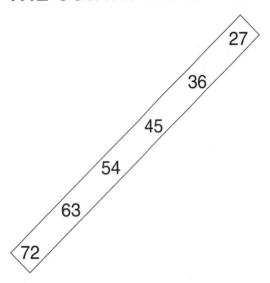

Fig. 9.11. The Octave Triad Family

Find the Octave Triad Family on the Palette Chart. They are in the clear diagonal box. The triads in the Octave Family are simply an octave with another interval attached. George Benson loves these, and they are a cool way to support a melody line. Don't forget to make templates of these seeds of the Palette Chart on all possible string sets.

Here is the ⧈63 seed along the A, G, and B strings.

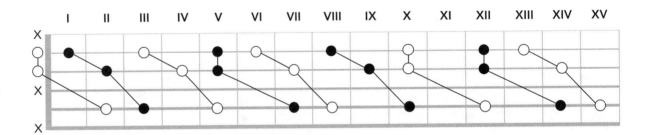

Fig. 9.12. 63 Seeds along the A, G, and B Strings

 I like these 63 seeds with this Latin groove and I really like the Cluster Family seeds and the Quartal Family seeds. How can I use them with chord symbols?

Good question, Chester. For a 3-note seed to begin to reflect and relate to a chord symbol's quality, the seed should include guide tones. With this in mind, here is something I call "The Seeds from Chord Symbols Dictionary."

THE SEEDS-FROM-CHORD-SYMBOLS DICTIONARY

For this seeds dictionary, I started with a seed template for major quality chord symbols: symbols such as Maj7, Maj7(9), Maj7(6), Maj7(♯11), Maj6(9). Let me show you how I organized the possibilities.

Starting with the Major Quality Template, I simply took each Palette Chart seed and built around one of the chord quality's guide tones (the 3rd and/or 7th degrees). For organization, I began by putting the 3rd degree—in this case, an E natural for C major quality—as the bottom note of a seed, then as the middle note of the seed, and then as the top note of the seed.

So here, Chester, are some possibilities from the Cluster and Quartal Families using the above search technique. I have put the guide tone—in this case, the 3rd degree—in bold type, for reference.

Some Seeds from Symbols with Cluster Family for C Major Quality

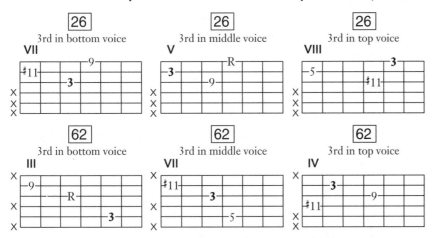

Fig. 9.13. Some Seeds from Symbols with Cluster Family for C Major Quality

Some Seeds from Symbols with Quartal Family for C Major Quality

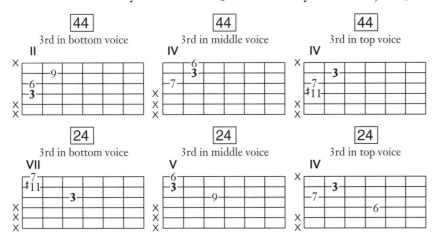

Fig. 9.14. Some Seeds from Symbols with Quartal Family for C Major Quality

To complete my Seeds from Chord Symbols Dictionary, I have done this process with all the seeds, in major quality, as we have started above, and also in the minor, dominant 7th, and −7♭5 qualities.

Also use the 7th degree as a possible focal point to build the seeds from, especially with the dominant 7th quality. In the case of –7♭5, you may find the flat 5th degree a nice building block.

Say Jon, show us some of the Palette Chart possibilities in action with some chord symbols!

Okay Chester, here is the progression of "Giant Strides" with a real mix of 3-note possibilities. Just about every family is used!

The guide tones are in clear diamonds for reference, here. Traditional notation shows the direction freedom that 3-note seeds give us. Note the arrows to indicate contrary motion in the size of the seeds, from small to larger and vice versa. "The Seeds from Chord Symbols Dictionary" really helps in finding possibilities.

This chapter was just a dip into the Palette Chart to help include more 3-note possibilities in our dictionary-building process. *The Guitarist's Guide to Composing and Improvising* is again chock-full of ideas that tap into these 3-note chord families. So here's "Giant Strides."

GIANT STRIDES
WITH 3-NOTE VOICINGS FROM THE PALETTE CHART

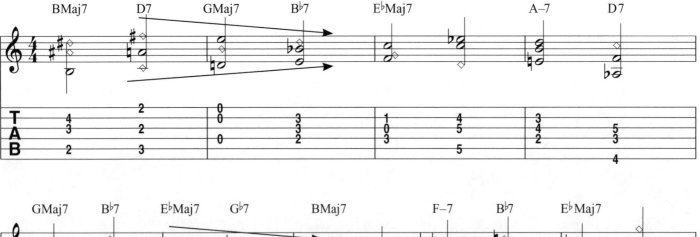

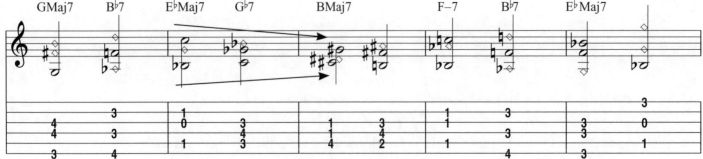

Fig. 9.15. "Giant Strides" with 3-Note Voicings

CHAPTER 10: TAKING OFF

EXPLORING AND CHALLENGING OUR CHORD VOCABULARY

Here in the "Taking Off" chapter are studies that challenge our chord vocabulary—to test our dictionary and to help us find new forms. As if we haven't enough already!

Back in the "Foundations" chapter, we met Mr. B., the cat who could really deliver an accompaniment with a groove. His accompaniment was beautiful—not only rhythmically, but also dynamically. He never played too loudly or too softly. Also, he supported melodies with chords whose top voices really supported the lead lines. Sometimes, he would use the melody note itself on the top of a chord or perhaps "answer" the melody as a canon or move in contrary motion to the melody. He could also play beautiful *chord solos*—the melody of a tune harmonized with chords.

In order to do any of these powerful techniques, a solid vocabulary and ability to support any lead note with any quality of chord is essential. Here are some studies that focus on the top voice of our chord forms to add to our accompaniment abilities, as well as soloing with chords.

STEP COMP

"Gimme some block chords, Red...."

— Miles Davis, from the recording of "You're My Everything" from
the classic album *Relaxin' with the Miles Davis Quintet*
(Prestige 7129, 1956/Remastered 2006)

I practice Step Comp on a regular basis to stay sharp with harmonizing lead voices and also to find new voicing possibilities. In Step Comp, you choose a chord progression for study. As you progress from chord to chord, move the top voice by step—in scale-wise motion to the next possible harmonizable note, which may be a basic chord tone or tension of the next chord.

An awareness of how a chord is functioning in a progression will detail tension possibilities. Dominant 7th chords will have the most tension variability, and back on the fifth floor, I gave some tension possibilities for dominant 7th chords. Please review this information, if needed, especially the Bright/Dark Chart (see figure 5.3).

What did Miles mean by "block chords?"

In the recording, Red Garland (the pianist) first began the introduction of "You're My Everything" using chords in his left hand and a single-note, rhythmically independent melodic line in his right hand. Miles then whistled sharply, interrupting, and said, "Gimme some block chords, Red, block chords." Red then restarted the intro with chords in both hands, moving in the same rhythm, as "blocks" of notes.

LET'S TRY STEP COMP

What does "comp" mean?

"Comp" is short for "accompaniment," Chester.

1. First, choose a chord progression to work with. I have chosen the standard tune "Autumn Leaves" for illustration, since the progression displays both major and minor keys and their dominant 7th chords. See figure 10.1 below.

2. Play the first chord of the progression however you wish, anywhere on the fretboard, with the top note of the chord on the high E string or the B string. In the opening bar of "Autumn Leaves," I chose to start with E natural on the B string as the lead note (top voice) for the A–7 chord. It is the 5th degree of the A–7 chord.

3. Choose a direction, up or down, to continue. Let's go up for now.

   Since the next chord is D7—a dominant 7th chord that is moving cycle V to the GMaj7 chord—the next possible lead note moving up is F natural, the sharp 9th tension on the D7. I used a voicing for a D7(♯9,♭13).

4. For the next chord, GMaj7, the F natural of the D7(♯9) will move up to the F♯, the 7th degree of GMaj7. Since our dictionary templates are detailed with chord degrees on specific strings, finding an appropriate chord form and quality to support a lead note will be easy.

Be patient. As you do Step Comp on your own, you will notice repetition of possibilities. This is how this skill of harmonizing melodies with chords is attained: bit by bit.

Next, the F♯ lead voice of the GMaj7 chord moves to the G (the 5th degree of the CMaj7 chord), and then moves to A natural, the 3rd degree of the F♯–7♭5 chord.

The next possible note will be the B natural, the root of the B7 chord. Since this is a basic chord tone, notice that I have used a tension, ♭13, in the second voice, since the dominant 7th chord is moving cycle V to an E minor chord. When basic chord tones are a lead voice, especially on dominant 7th chords, try to include a tension quality in one of the lower voices to give color to the 4-part dominant 7th chord.

This first example of Step Comp ends with the C♯, the 6th degree in the lead of the E minor 6(9) chord voicing. To continue the study, move the lead voice as high up the E string as possible. Then come down, moving to the low end of the B string. This example just gets us started. Use any steady rhythmic value you wish for these studies.

"STEP COMP WITH AUTUMN LEAVES"

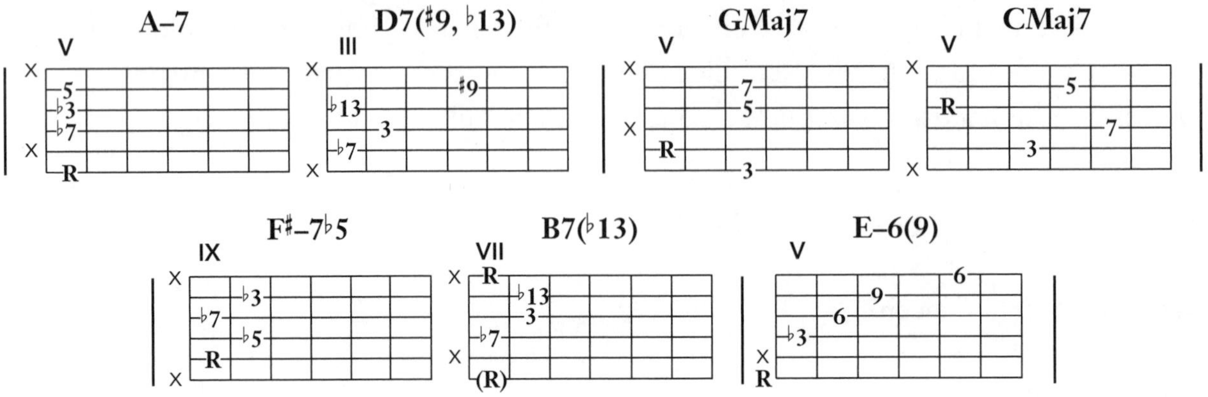

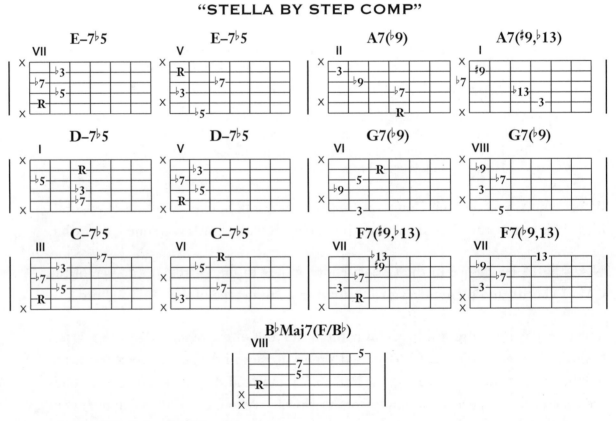

Fig. 10.1. "Step Comp with Autumn Leaves"

Now, here is another example of Step Comp, an excerpt from a study I call "Stella by Step Comp." I have thrown in a variety of possibilities, including an open-string voicing, a slash chord, and some incomplete dominant 7th voicings. Here, I began in a downward direction, moving the lead voice to the low end of the B string and then reversing direction, gradually moving the lead voice to the high end of the high E string.

"STELLA BY STEP COMP"

Fig. 10.2. "Stella by Step Comp"

As you Step Comp, you may tire of using the same chord grips for certain lead notes. With the help of your dictionary, find more possibilities to give you more choices.

These next two studies, "Common-Tone Comp" and especially "Common-Tone Comp *Extra-Strength*," may help you find other possibilities for harmonizing lead notes.

How can I remember all these new voicings?

Remember, Chester, that 97.8 percent of the new voicings you find can be plugged into a simple II V I progression. As we have seen during construction, using new vocabulary in context helps you to digest new information into your harmonic belly.

COMMON-TONE COMP

In Common-Tone Comp, as in Step Comp, a chord progression is used to study harmonizing lead voices. Here in Common-Tone Comp, the lead voice of the first chord is used as long as possible as the lead voice through the rest of the chord progression. If the lead note must move, move it to the nearest possible lead note.

Here in figure 10.3 is Common-Tone Comp with "Autumn Leaves." Let's start with the same starting chord form for the A–7 chord. The lead voice is E natural, the 5th degree of the A–7 chord. That same note E becomes the 9th degree of the D7 chord, which becomes the tension 6th degree of the GMaj7 chord, then the 3rd degree of CMaj7, and then ♭7th of the F♯–7♭5 chord. But then, it must move for the B7(♭9) chord. I will shift it down a fret to become D♯, the 3rd degree of the B7 chord. Notice the ♭9th of B7(♭9), the note C. This dark tension leads to the E minor (9) chord, on which I used a sexy open-string chord form. The lead note returns to E natural, the root of the E minor chord.

COMMON-TONE COMP WITH "AUTUMN LEAVES"

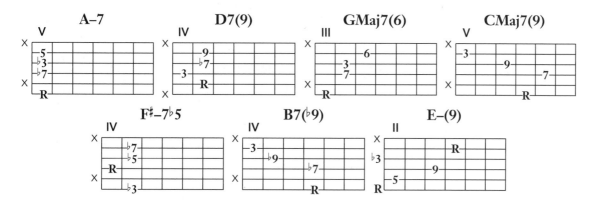

Fig. 10.3. Common-Tone Comp with "Autumn Leaves"

COMMON-TONE COMP *EXTRA STRENGTH!*

As you can tell, searching for the bigger, better, cooler-than-the-last-chord-I-found chord has always been fun for me. The only difference here in Common-Tone Comp *Extra Strength* is that one consistent finger and string will be used to finger the top voice or highest note pitch-wise of each chord of a progression. That top voice (note) and *assigned finger and string* will be used as long as possible, harmonically. The physical limitation of using a consistent finger will open up possibilities we may not have seen or thought of otherwise. When doing this study, I always think of Django Reinhardt—one of the great guitarists, who had only two usable fingers on his fingerboard hand! He used this physical limitation to create a totally unique approach to playing the guitar.

1. First, choose any chord progression for study. Play the first chord anywhere, however you wish. Note which finger you are using for the top voice. This finger will be used for the top voice of *each* chord in the progression.

2. Keep the same top voice for each chord, if possible, harmonically. If the top voice must move for harmonic reasons, usually a shift of one fret will do it, but continue to use the same finger for the top voice. Having the "limitation" of the *same finger* on that top voice will force you to break down that "muscle memory" of the same old chord forms.

3. Be inventive. Try open strings, for finding new possibilities. In your explorations, you don't have to play every note of the chord. Just be careful not to lose the basic quality and function of the chord you are exploring.

For this introduction to Common-Tone Comp *Extra Strength*, let's use a simple 2-bar progression, a I VI II V progression in the key of C major. This example keeps the first finger (index finger) of my fingerboard hand on the lead voice. For now, I will move through the progression twice. Even in this simple example, I have found some nice new possibilities, thanks to open strings and the fact that I am using a limitation—the same finger for the lead voice. Again, a limitation opens up unlimited possibilities!

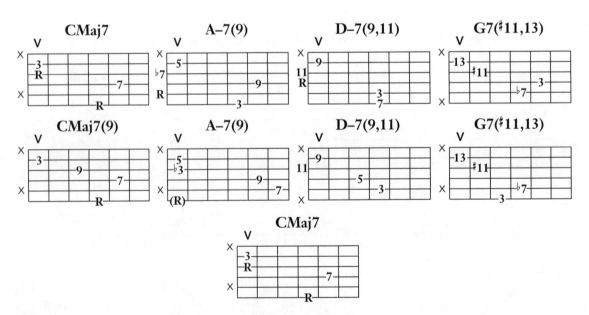

Fig. 10.4. Common-Tone Comp *Extra Strength* with I VI II V, Played with the First Finger

Here is another example, but now with the fourth finger as lead-voice finger. I could have used more obvious, common voicings with this lead finger, but stretched my possibilities instead. Literally!

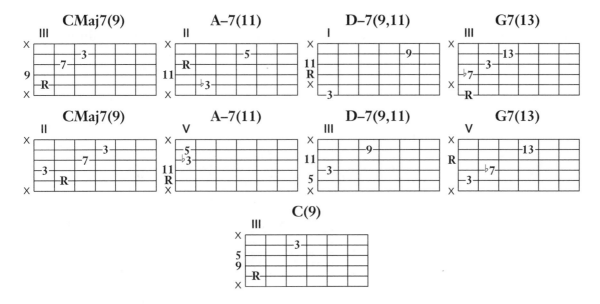

Fig. 10.5. Common-Tone Comp *Extra Strength* with I VI II V Using the Fourth Finger

So much depends on location of the lead voice and using a consistent finger. In these examples, the lead voice (E natural) is on the B string. If I used the high open E string for the lead, then the voicing possibilities become totally different. Give it a try!

APPROACH-NOTE VOICING

Approach-Note Voicing is a simple concept that adds interest to standard chord voicings. In this technique, individual notes of a chord structure are approached either chromatically, by half step, or by a whole step.

Take any chord form, and see how many ways you can move into a note of the chord, from below or from above. Your chording-hand fingers have to be inventive with this technique, and your strumming hand may sometimes have to use a finger-style technique.

Here are three variations on a I VI II V progression in the key of C. On the template, a solid circle with an arrow indicates an approach note and its direction of movement into the chord.

In your dictionary, you have been compiling "blocks" of harmonic sounds, which in general, are played in that manner: a block of notes moving to another block of notes all at the same time. This block-like texture is called *homophonic texture*. Harmony can also be produced with single, independently moving notes. That texture is called *poly-*

phonic texture, which is what this technique suggests, with the independent approach note. Many folks would call this a more contrapuntal approach. In fact, as the chord sustains, move the approach note into position, rhythmically by itself, independently.

Counterpoint is an essential focus throughout my first book, *The Guitarist's Guide to Composing and Improvising*. This technique is the tip of the iceberg of possibilities!

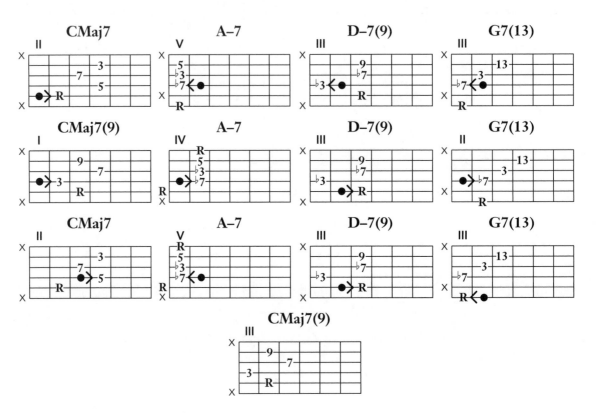

Fig. 10.6. Approach-Note Voicings

THE CHORD SOLO

All the chord vocabulary we have built together will help us in many ways, including Chord Soloing technique—supporting the melodies of tunes with voicings. To demonstrate this technique, grab any tune book. Take the tunes' melodic lines and *harmonize* them—"thicken" a melody note with notes from the respective chord symbol. Remember that your dictionary has easy references for chord qualities, degrees, and strings already built in.

Since it is winter holiday season as I am writing this section, I have chosen a bit of an old favorite for this next example, in figure 10.7. It should be easy to tell what tune it is. I have harmonized every note with a chord, for study sake, but in practice, you don't need to harmonize them all.

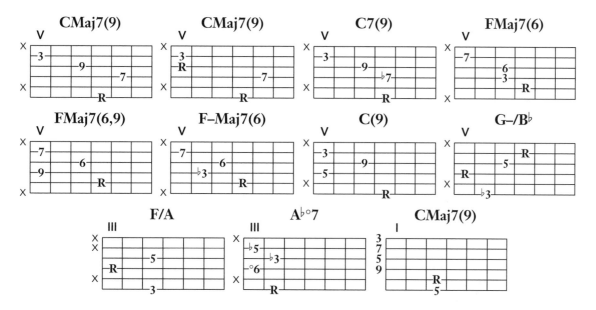

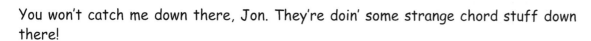

Fig. 10.7. Happy Holidays

This simple tune usually has simple chords. Where did you get those "extra" chords, Jon??

Chester, they are the result of a combination of working in an effective bass line (bottom voice), along with various approach chords, and trial and error. And hoping they produce something musical.

The preceding studies will challenge and invigorate your chord vocabulary. Remember that with any search, sometimes you find the gold and sometimes not. Be patient, and you will find voicings you may have never found otherwise.

And Chester, I may need you later, down in the Research and Development Lab.

You won't catch me down there, Jon. They're doin' some strange chord stuff down there!

CHAPTER 11: THE RESEARCH AND DEVELOPMENT LAB

XI

Down here in the Research and Development Lab, I will share with you some ideas that are "works in progress." I would love to hear your feedback and suggestions on these projects. Please contact me if you have any ideas concerning these works. You never know what harmonic oddities may bubble up here! Even Chester, chord explorer that he is, chickened out, the wim…..

Hold it Jon, here I am. I couldn't miss this!

Nice to see you, Chester. I could use some help down here!

"Music either rests or doesn't rest."

I always thought that Olivier Messiaen, a great composer, said this, but I can't guarantee it! I know the quote may sound like an obvious statement, but for me, the words powerfully open up a more liberal approach to comprovising with music and exploring harmonic possibilities. I actually realized that I now have a love/hate relationship with chord symbols. I enjoy using them musically, as necessary reference points as a composer and performer, but I also realize that they can create blinders that can hide possibilities.

BEYOND THE CHORD SYMBOL

As we have seen, the chord symbol is a handy way to portray a composer's harmonic intentions in popular music. From bebop to Zappa, the chord-symbol language is a mainstay in popular music composition technique. Although a rich language, chord symbology is a limited one. The majority of music on planet Earth exists entirely *without* chord symbology as a part of its language. The traditional musics of India and Java, China and Japan, Aboriginal music, and the modern ages of Western European classical music composition do not use chord symbols! And that's a lot of music. In fact, think of the music that we produced as early guitarists in dusty garages. Pure sound. Chord symbols were the farthest thing from our minds. "Hey, that works! That doesn't!" In fact, a lot more seemed to work for us back in those days. Gets ya thinkin', doesn't it?

Due to its limitations, chord symbol language cannot be used to translate these "other" musics of the world. The harmonic possibilities are just too vast.

In India, the harmonic intervallic interaction of the sitar's melodic line against the drone of the tambura. In the deep African rain forest, Pygmys performing complex vocalizations, a Japanese shamisen accompanying several voices, a Bartók string quartet—the list is endless. No chord symbols!

Here are three concepts I use to create a series of harmonies that do not use traditional chord-symbol thinking. For me, they have opened up some new harmonic comprovisational possibilities.

TONAL STUDY 1. TO REST OR NON-REST? THAT IS THE DIATONIC QUESTION.

For this first concept, let's take that opening quote, "Music either rests or doesn't rest," quite literally. As mentioned earlier, several factors come into play in creating musical cadence; tonality, rhythm, and dynamics, to name a few. In this study, we will focus on tonality to create a basic series of notes. How one would breathe musical life into this harmonic series rhythmically, dynamically, etc. is up to the individual comproviser.

In traditional harmony classes, labels are used to basically analyze different levels of cadence in harmonic progressions: T for restful points in a progression, SD for subdominant, D for dominant, and SDM for subdominant minor, non-restful points in a progression. Here in this first technique, only two will be used: R for restful and NR for non-restful. Remember that here in the Research and Development Lab, we are experimenting. We will find ideas that are quite unique, so don't be miffed if they don't fit neatly into your idiomatic expectations.

For starters, let's work in user-friendly C major tonality. Taking the notes of a C major scale, we can build a restful (R) sounding chord using any notes of the scale *except* the F note. The insertion of an F note (or 4th degree of the C major scale) creates a non-rest (NR) chord.

In the following progression, note how the introduction of the F note creates the movement to non-rest (NR). Now, you will recognize and could label some of these structures with a common chord symbol if you wish, but the point here is the pure rest/non-rest concept. It will open up many possibilities that chord-symbol thinking would not.

TONAL STUDY 1

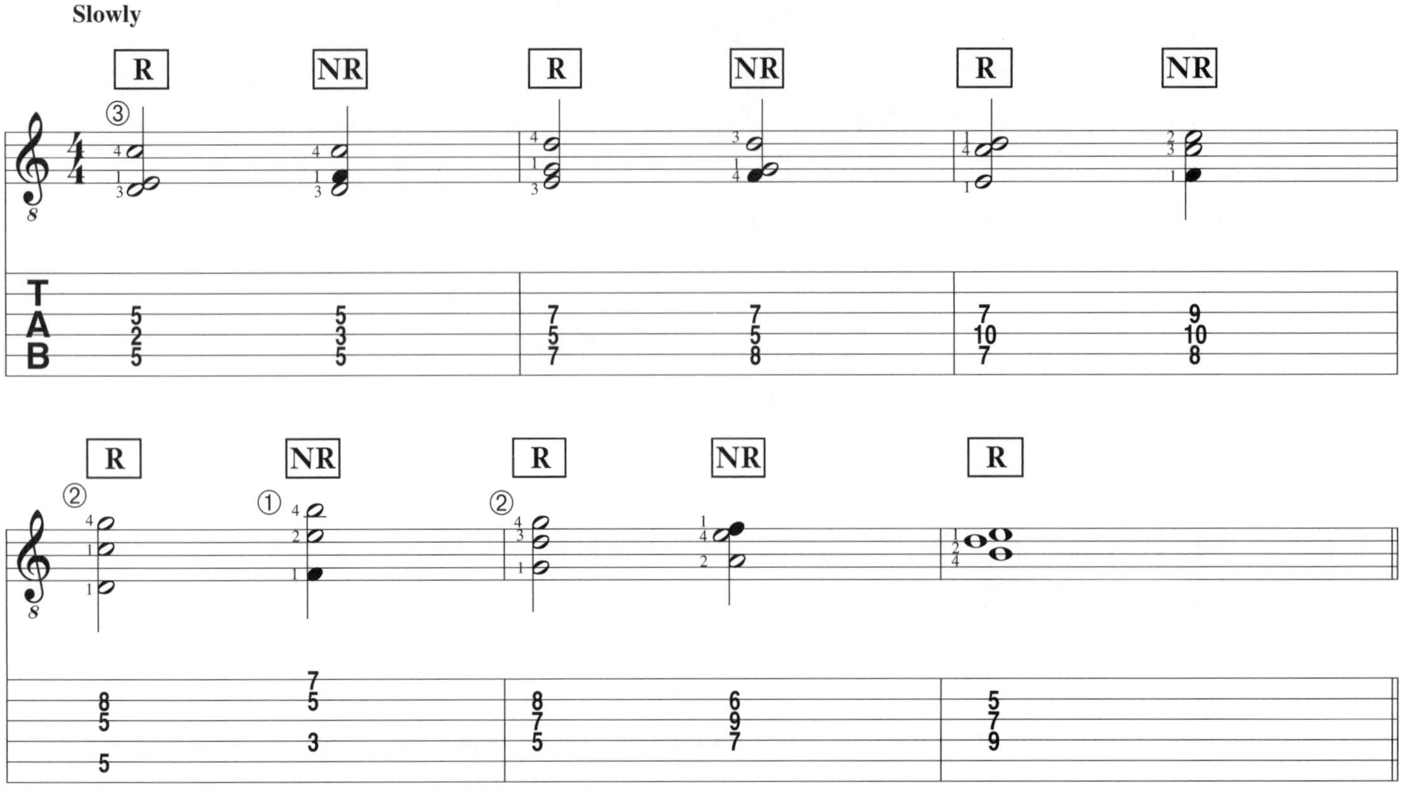

Fig. 11.1. Tonal Study 1: To Rest or Non-Rest? That is the Diatonic Question.

It's nice to get away from the chord symbols for a bit.

This stuff stretches the imagination, Chester.

TONAL STUDY 2. TO REST OR NON-REST? THAT IS THE CHROMATIC QUESTION.

Now, let's open up the entire chromatic scale for our work. Again, all C major scale notes except the F(!) will be used for R (Restful) chord structures. But here, any note(s) not in the C major scale may be added and used to create a NR (Non-Restful) chord. Try any rest/non-rest patterns you wish. Vincent Persechetti would!

TONAL STUDY 2

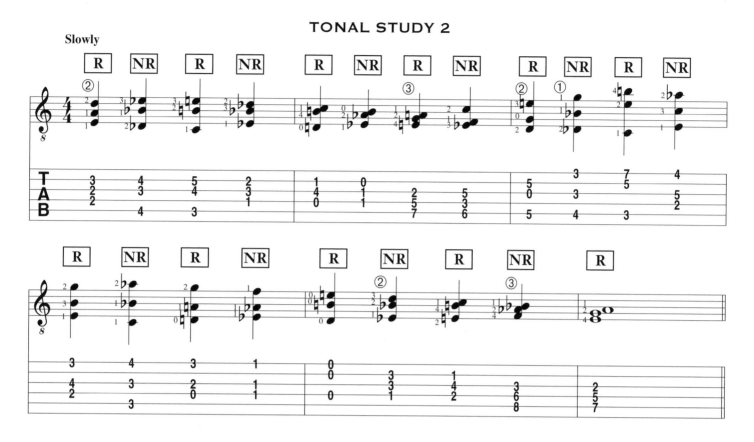

Fig. 11.2. Tonal Study 2: To Rest or Non-Rest? That is the *Chromatic* Question.

Now that's getting a bit too far out for me, Jon.

Hang in there, Chester. It is like developing a taste for fine wine or cheese.

I'll stick with the Velveeta, big boy.

Remember Chester, these ideas are simply catalysts for your imagination. How you use them is up to your aesthetic decision.

THE SUPERDUPERDOUBLEWHAMMYCHROMIUMPLATINUMCHART (SDDWCPC)

Able to leap tall buildings in a single bound!!

In our construction process, we have used pure interval thinking—simple music architecture to gain a deeper understanding. Intervals exist in the harmonic texture of any world-music language. As we have seen, a major part of harmonic progression or cadence is interval interaction. All music has another common element: the natural occurrence of *overtones*—the harmonic or overtone series, which rules the interaction of tones and harmonic progressions (see chapter 1). Also, music has basic sound dimensions: dynamics, rhythm, direction, articulation, and timbre, which are strong elements in a cadence or progression of musical ideas. And they can actually reverse a cadence. That placid, restful major triad can easily become restless with an aggressive use of volume and orchestration. That rich cluster of minor seconds can sound quite docile when played softly. Since this is a harmonic treatise we are building, here in the Research and Development Lab, I will offer some harmonic progression ideas that move beyond traditional chord-symbol thinking. How you deliver these ideas musically is up to you, and rightly so.

You're scaring me, Jon!

Don't worry, Chester, exploration is fun, and we'll find some harmonic goodies that the chord-symbol language might not have suggested.

As we have seen and heard, intervals have qualities of rest or non-rest in relation to one another and to tonality. A major second when heard next to a perfect fifth will have a more intense quality, but next to a minor second, it will have a less intense quality. With this basic tenet in mind, we can observe harmonic structure by pure interval intensity and create a series of cadences or progressions relative to these intensities.

We looked at 3-note harmonic structures in chapter 3 and in the Palette Chart section. Now, let's take a brief look at *all* possible 3-note structures.

In the Palette Chart (see figure 9.1), 3-note chords are explored diatonically, built using traditional tonal scales. To be inclusive, we will now use one scale, the chromatic scale, to search for 3-note possibilities. To describe the 3-note structures, I will use the two-number system, as with the Palette Chart, except now specific intervals will be indicated.

$\boxed{-2,P5}$ refers to a triad that is built from a minor second and a perfect fifth. You can use any note to build from. That is up to you. Here is one possible example.

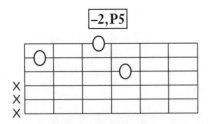

Fig. 11.3. Minor Second/Perfect Fifth 3-Note Structure

Hey, more chord symbols!

Yes, Chester, but they are not tonally exclusive and include all interval possibilities, essentially.

For my own work, I have taken 3-note harmonic structures and placed them in order from consonance to dissonance. Of course, intensity is a subjective issue, so my order of chords from consonance to dissonance will be different than yours. I actually built mine using the overtone series. My chart is not perfect, but I use it, and it really helps me to produce some very interesting harmonic ideas. I have built my chart to read from left to right moving from the most consonant 3-note chord to the most dissonant one.

Here are my first (most consonant) and last (most dissonant) structures. The dots represent all the other 3-note structures between these two extreme points.

And there are quite a few. From each seed from the Palette Chart, there are basically four possibilities. From ㉒ alone, you can have:

| –2,–2 | –2,2 | 2,2 | 2,–2 |

In total, approximately 144 3-note structures! And that is not counting all possible pitches!

Yikes!

I have given my entire SDDWCPC to folks and have always had feedback such as, "I really feel that this seed is not as consonant as you think." So, to save both of us agita, you create your own SDDWCPC.

Now remember, you don't have to build this chart! As you can tell by now, I am a chord junkie and a curious composer and improviser, and I particularly enjoy alternative ways of creating music. Even if you simply become more aware of a structure's essential interval intensity when creating a harmonic progression, it will add possibilities for you. Anyway, I love my chart and call it:

THE SUPERDUPERDOUBLEWHAMMYCHROMIUMPLATINUMCHART

Here is a simple musical example using my chart. The example uses a basic 3-chord blues progression as a cadence guide. The example is not intended to sound like or be a blues progression. Simply, the restful or "I chord" structure used would be found on my SuperDuper... chart somewhere to the left in intensity of the "IV chord" structure. The "V chord" structure would be to the right, in intensity.

Here is the progression stated in a most simple manner with simple rhythm and clearly labeled with interval description.

SUPERDUPERDOUBLEWHAMMYCHROMIUMPLATINUM CHART STUDY 1
USING A BASIC BLUES FORM

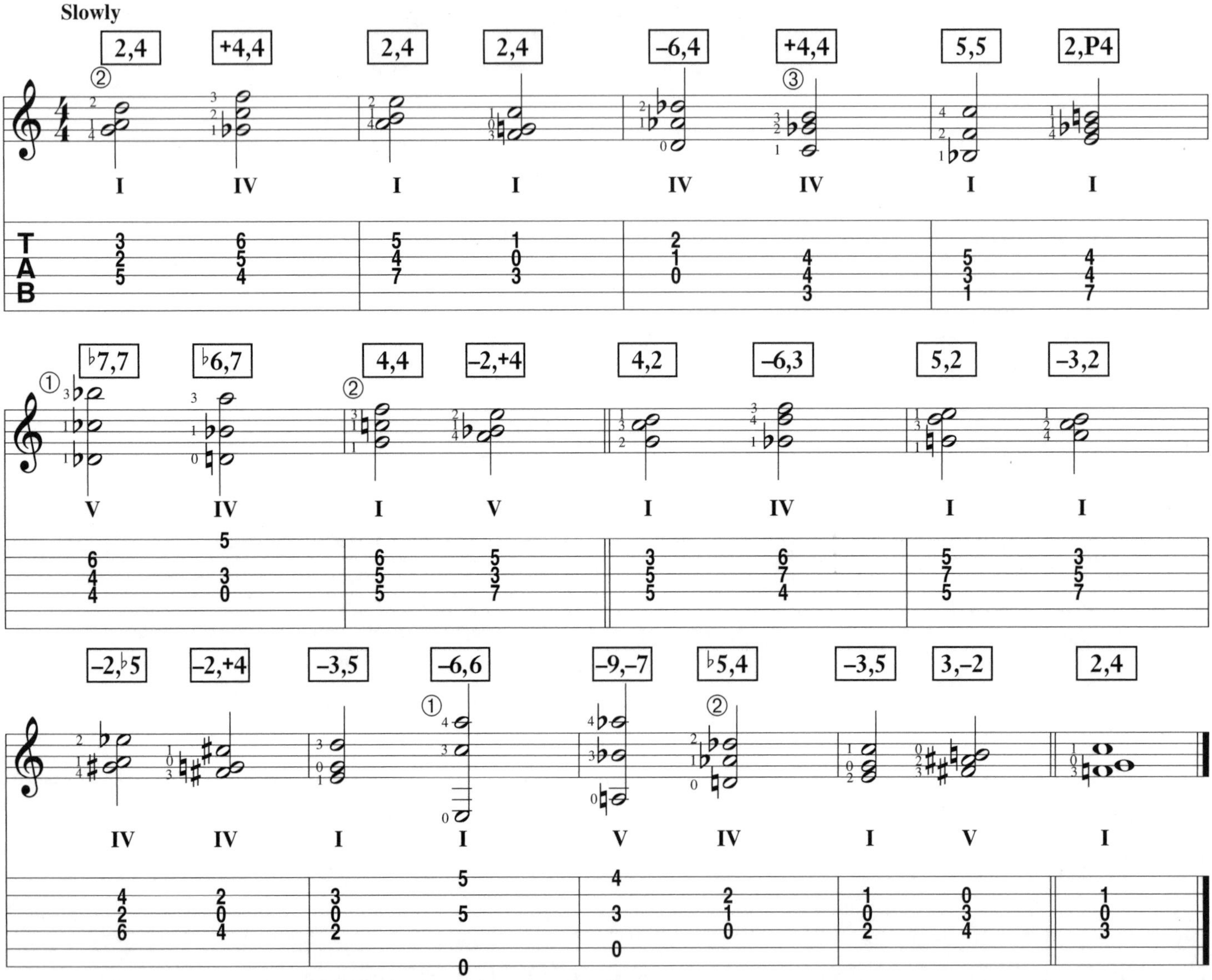

Fig. 11.4 SuperDuperDoubleWhammyBlues

I like that one.

Care for a piece of Parmagiano Reggiano and some Chianti?

Now you're pushing it, Jon.

My next project really needs your help and is:

THE CHORD SYMBOL ACADEMY AWARDS!!!

Just for fun, I wanted to give a little back to all those chord symbols that have helped me make a living over the past too many years to say! So I thought that a Chord Symbol Academy Awards would be fun to have: finding the three most-used chord symbols used by peoplekind. But I need help!!

All you need to do is count how many times one particular chord symbol occurs in the *Real Book*. Don't forget to take repeats! Count how many times the actual symbol is played in one chorus.

Send me back a message saying you would like to participate, and I will send you a chord symbol to count.

Also jot down your guess of the first, second, and third place most-popular chord symbol winners! I will send you back the results.

Thanks.

I actually enjoyed that visit to the R&D lab. My guess would be an F7 chord for the Chord Symbol Academy Award winner.

Really, Chester? Interesting.

The following chapters, "The Break Room," and "The Tool Box," are support and reference chapters referred to throughout the book. Our official dictionary-building project is just about complete, for now.

Here in the "The Break Room" chapter, you will find several activities to try during your breaks from your dictionary building. You can try The Chord Symbols CrossTones Puzzle, or some yoga stretches to help your hands and arms through the workouts of playing this great instrument or have fun with the Incredible Time-Machine Study.

Hi Jon!

Hi Chester. Nice to see you here in the Break Room. I guess you needed a break, too.

Yea. Nice to relax. Say Jon, I've got a good one for you!

Shoot, Chester.

How many lead guitar players does it take to change a light bulb?

Ya got me.

It only takes one. One to hold on to the light bulb as the rest of the world revolves around him.

Good one, Chester.

One more quick one, Jon. What do you call a guitar player that only knows two chords?

Got me again.

A music critic.

Wanna try some yoga, Chester? It really helps!

Sure.

YOGA FOR THE HARD-WORKING CHORD EXPLORER

Playing the guitar is pretty strenuous stuff for our hands and arms. Some of the chord forms we come across during our harmonic explorations can present challenges for our bodies.

Through my study of yoga over the past several years, I have gleaned some simple routines that work well for me as warm-ups to prepare for performance and for general hand and arm flexibility. Here are two of them. Try them before and after playing. These do not replace your gentle playing warm-ups that I hope you do prior to any playing session.

THE PRAYER POSE

The word prayer simply indicates the starting position of the hands.

1. Find a comfortable sitting position and maintain a straight back throughout the pose.

2. Place your hands in a simple prayer position, palms touching, fingertips pointing up, directly in front of your sternum. Raise your elbows until your forearms are parallel to the floor. Keep your shoulders relaxed.

3. Take a slow, full, deep breath in. Breathe through your nose only.

4. When you slowly exhale, move your hands to the right, gently pushing your right hand with your left hand slowly, maintaining your forearms parallel to the floor. Do *not* overexert or overstretch your arms and wrists as you move them as fully and comfortably possible to the right.

5. With your next slow, full, deep breath in, slowly bring your hands back to center.

6. On your next out breath gently push your left hand with your right hand, again maintaining a forearm position parallel to the floor, as you slowly move your hands to the left along with your out breath.

7. With your next breath in, bring your hands back to center.

Continue this cycle, focusing on your breath.

Do not overexert your hands and arms. You should feel a gentle stretching—a nice massage this pose is creating for you. Try five cycles at first.

THE BEGGING POSE

1. Stand, and maintain a straight back throughout the pose.

2. Place hands together in prayer pose, but now weave your fingers together and bend them, creating a begging posture.

3. Take a slow, full, deep breath. Remember to breathe through your nose. As you breathe out, push your hands downward, letting your wrists slowly separate, maintaining the weave of your fingers and creating a nice gentle stretch as you straighten your arms downward towards the floor.

4. Maintaining this straight armed posture, on your in breath, slowly swing your hands and arms in front of you, gradually to be straight up over your head. Continue to relax your shoulders downward as you stretch your hands upward.

5. Exhale slowly and swing your hands and arms downward to the bottom position.

6. Continue this cycle. Do not overexert, and move gently and comfortably with your breath. Again, start with five cycles.

I hope these two exercises help your hands and arms maintain health throughout the physical workouts of our everyday playing and chord explorations.

THE CHORD SYMBOLS CROSSTONES PUZZLE

Now, try your luck with the Chord Symbols CrossTones Puzzle. Try timing yourself! It works like any crossword puzzle, but now your "hints" are chord symbols.

Just to get you started, I sketched in the answer to 1 Across. The rest is up to you!

That was nice of you, Chester.

As they say in the bakery business, "That's the yeast I could do!"

Nasty one, Chester.

THE CHORD SYMBOLS CROSSTONES PUZZLE
A Challenge for Your Chord Spelling

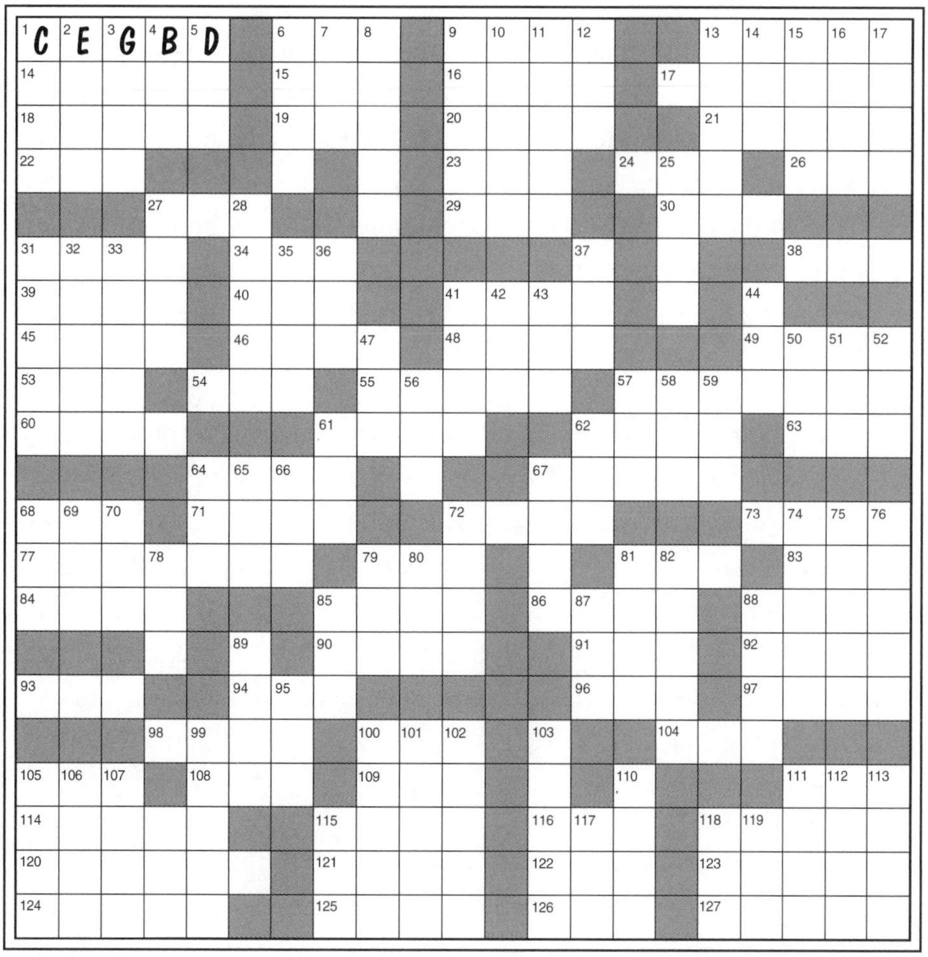

Fig. 12.1. The Chord Symbols CrossTones Puzzle

ACROSS

1	CMaj7(9)
6	F
9	B♭–7
13	D7(9)
14	E♭Maj7(9)
15	A♭
16	D–7
17	D♭Maj7♯5(9, ♯11)
18	G♭Maj7(9)
19	C–
20	F–Maj7
21	A–7(9)
22	B♭°
23	A°
24	F–
26	G–
27	F♯°
29	C–
30	C
31	B–7♭5
34	E♭+
37	C–(Second Inversion)
38	G♭
39	D7
40	G
41	C7
45	F♯–7♭5
46	B°7
48	E♭Maj7
49	D7
53	A–
54	B♭+
55	C7♭5(9)
57	G7(9, ♯11, 13)
60	C♯–7♭5
61	C7♯5
62	GMaj7
63	D
64	F7
67	G–7(9)
68	G♭
71	A♭Maj7
72	E♭–Maj7
73	E♭–7
77	B♭7(9, ♯11, 13)
79	C°
81	A♭+
83	B♭
84	D–7♭5
85	C7
86	F♯–7♭5
88	B♭–7
90	E°7
91	C–
92	D♭Maj7
93	G♭
94	D–
96	E°
97	F–7♭5
98	B°7
100	E♭

104	D–
105	E♭+
108	F♯°
109	G–
111	A♭
114	G7(9)
115	G♭7
116	E♭
118	FMaj7(9)
120	B♭7(9, ♯11)
121	B♭7
122	G
123	AMaj7(9)
124	DMaj7(9)
125	D♭Maj7♯5
126	B♭
127	C7(9)

DOWN

1	C–7♭5
2	E°7
3	G°7
4	B°
5	D°
6	F–Maj7
7	A°
8	C–7(9)
9	B♭Maj7(9)
10	D♭Maj7(9)
11	F7(9)
12	A♭+
13	D–7(9)
14	F♯°
15	A–7
16	C–7
17	E–7
25	A♭Maj7
27	F♯–7♭5
28	C–Maj7(9)
31	B–7(9)
32	D7(9)
33	FMaj7(9)
35	GMaj7
36	B°
37	G–
41	C–7♭5
42	E°
43	G–
44	B♭
47	A♭+
50	D (First Inversion)
51	F♯–(First Inversion)
52	A–(First Inversion)
56	E
57	G
58	B°
59	D
61	C–
62	G–
64	F–
65	A–
66	C–
67	G–Maj7
68	G♭+
69	B♭
70	D♭
72	E♭–7
74	G♭Maj7(9)
75	B♭7(♭9)
76	D♭Maj7(9)
78	A♭+
79	C
80	E♭
81	A♭Maj7
82	C7(9)
85	A–(First Inversion)
87	A–
88	B♭–Maj7
89	B♭Maj7
95	F–
99	D7(9)
100	E♭Maj7(9)
101	G–7(9)
102	B♭7♭5(9)
103	A♭Maj7(9)
105	E♭Maj7(9)
106	GMaj7
107	B–7♭5
110	G♭Maj7♯5
111	A♭Maj7♯5
112	C7♯5
113	E♭Maj7♯5
115	G♭
117	G
118	F
119	A

THE INCREDIBLE TIME-MACHINE STUDY

Our growth and development as musicians are seldom as consistent as we would like. Some days, we ride the crest of our development cycle, with our confidence strong in our abilities. Other days, the downside makes us feel like we are not making any progress at all. I can safely say I've been riding this crazy rollercoaster of development longer than most of you, and have drawn some conclusions that may help smooth out the rest of your ride a bit. During what used to be my down days, I'd get depressed, beef about things, and gradually wait until the cycle turned for the better. It began to get tiring.

I began to notice that just before a down cycle hit, a significant musical trauma hit me first. I remember a conductor squawking at me, in front of the rest of a rather large orchestra, not to be mentioned here, that I was too loud and to turn down. A simple request, but crushing for my tender ego. But I did learn to respect dynamic markings a whole lot better, after that. Another time, I was performing with a dear friend, D. Sharpe. After finishing a set, he asked whether I was listening to him at all during the set. I lied, and said sure, but realized that I was so self-involved that I wasn't aware of the great ideas he was trying to feed me. Again, my ego was crushed, but my ensemble awareness sure took a turn for the better.

My greatest moments of musical enlightenment have occurred during many "sensitive" moments like these. I have come to realize that when that downside occurs, it is actually a positive sign that a light just went on, enabling me to view the next subject in my developmental progression more clearly. It simply means that my observation of a particular musical area has strengthened, enabling me to take another step forward. It took me a while to feel more positive about those downside days, but now that cycle isn't quite as topsy-turvy as it used to be. In fact, if I didn't have those downsides, I'd probably feel like a light went out, since now I realize that the downward swing is just giving me momentum to pop up to the next plateau.

Here's a simple fun thing to try, if you are feeling overwhelmed and in one of those slumps.

Did you ever feel like going back in time, for some crazy reason? Well, as guitar players, we're lucky because we can sort of do it.

Check this out. Let's say you hit one of those days when you feel like your progress has hit a brick wall. All the new ideas coming at you quickly here in *The Chord Factory* can do that to you!

To enter the time machine, simply take your guitar and reverse the whole kit 'n' caboodle. You are now holding the guitar so that your normal fingerboard hand is holding the pick and your other hand is fingering the notes and chords. The pegboard of the guitar is now facing east instead of west. Got it?

This really feels strange!

Of course, because this is a lot how it felt that first day you picked up this beast! You have gone back several years in time. Well, kinda….

Now, let's put you to work. First play something that has become pretty instinctive for you by now. Try a pentatonic scale. If you were holding your guitar regularly, this pentatonic scale would be something you could play while watching a movie and eating popcorn! But now, since you've taken a step back in time, your instinct is fairly useless. This simple pentatonic scale takes some real determination and intellect to figure out.

Try a simple chord progression. Play an F bar chord!

Wow! And ouch! I can still remember the shock of trying my first bar chord.

In time-machine mode, it's tough, but in regular mode we play these chords without a second thought.

It's simply because you've come a long way, baby! Many hours of practice, performance, hard work, determination, and intellectual ability have helped you make a technique become an instinctive ability. Some days, it's difficult to see progress because you are with yourself all the time (hopefully). It's tough to step back and gauge progress, since you are right up close to things. But when you take this simple step backwards in time, you will not only appreciate the progress you've made, but can also feel better about all the new intellectual techniques being thrown at you.

Eventually, with your continued hard work, these new techniques will also become part of your musical instinct.

Amazing! I've taken for granted how difficult it is to play this instrument!

You said it, Chester.

CHAPTER 14: TOOL BOX

Whoa, where is the 13th floor?

Not in this chord factory, Chester, it would be bad luck!

Here in the "Tool Box" chapter, you will find tools necessary for construction. Some templates you need: a blank chord template, the Major 7 Chord Template, some blank fingerboard templates, and a complete fingerboard template to check your work from chapter 1. Reference charts are also included here: an Interval Cross-Reference Chart and a Chord-Tones Cross-Reference Chart.

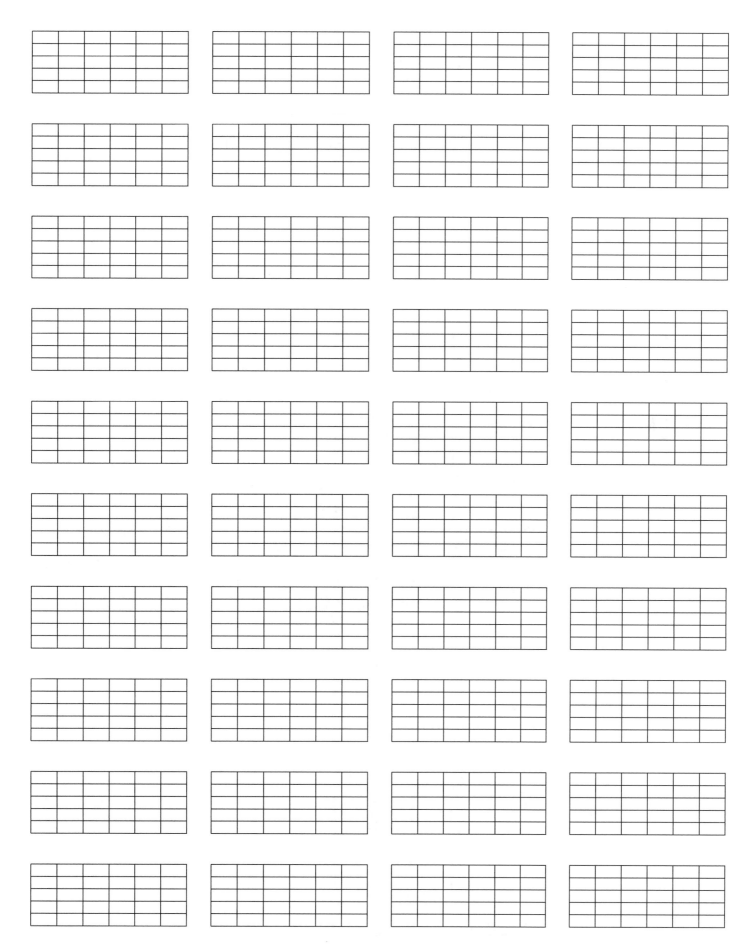

Fig. 14.1. Blank Chord Template

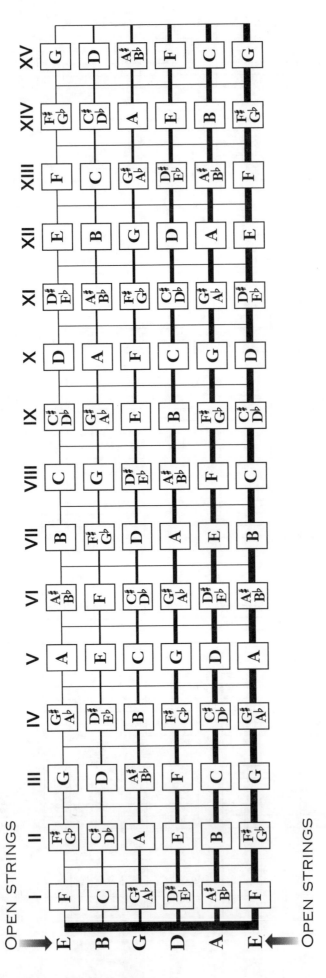

Fig. 14.2. The Fingerboard

FINGERBOARD TEMPLATES

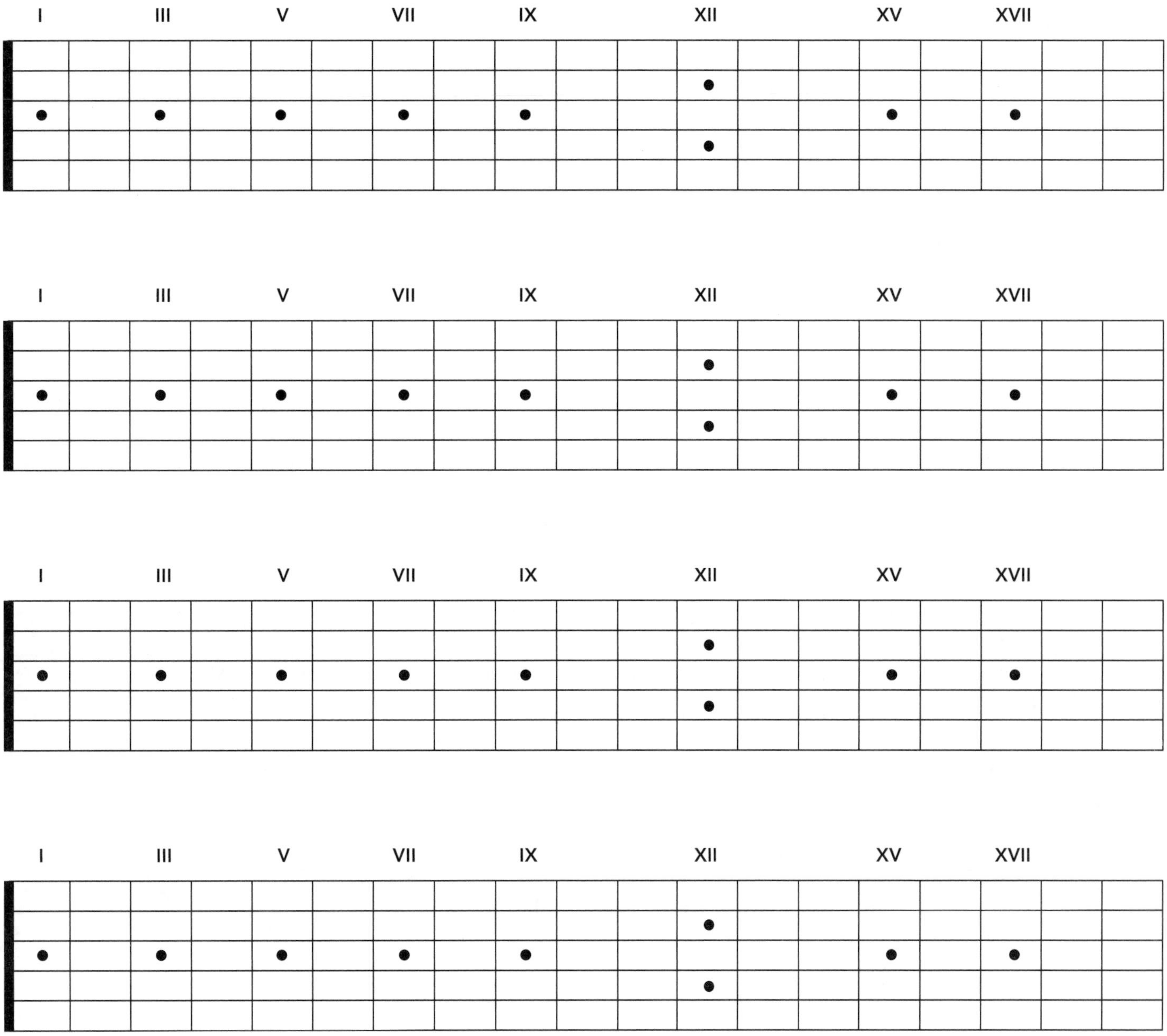

Fig. 14.3. Blank Fingerboard Templates

THE INTERVAL CROSS-REFERENCE CHART

Use this like a mileage chart! The left column contains the bottom note of an interval, and the top row contains interval qualities. If you want a major seventh above D, find the D in the left column, and then move along that row to the right until you are in the major seventh quality row, and you have your destination note! C#, the major seventh from D. Occasionally, I use enharmonic spellings to avoid double sharps and flats.

INTERVAL CROSS-REFERENCE CHART

	♭2	Maj2	♭3	Maj3	P4	#4	°5	P5	#5	♭6	Maj6	♭7	Maj7	8ve	♭9	Maj9	#9	10	11	#11	12	♭13	13
C	D♭	D	E♭	E	F	F#	G♭	G	G#	A♭	A	B♭	B	C	D♭	D	D#	E	F	F#	G	A♭	A
C#	D	D#	E	E#	F#	G	G	G#	A	A	A#	B	B#	C#	D	D#	E	E#	F#	G	G#	A	A#
D♭	D	E♭	F♭	F	G♭	G	G	A♭	A	A	B♭	C♭	C	D♭	D	E♭	E	F	G♭	G	A♭	A	B♭
D	E♭	E	F	F#	G	G#	A♭	A	A#	B♭	B	C	C#	D	E♭	E	F	F#	G	G#	A	B♭	B
D#	E	E#	F#	G	G#	A	A	A#	B	B	B#	C#	D	D#	E	E#	F#	G	G#	A	A#	B	B#
E♭	F♭	F	G♭	G	A♭	A	A	B♭	B	C♭	C	D♭	D	E♭	E	F	G♭	G	A♭	A	B♭	C♭	C
E	F	F#	G	G#	A	A#	B♭	B	B#	C	C#	D	D#	E	F	F#	G	G#	A	A#	B	C	C#
F	G♭	G	A♭	A	B♭	B	C♭	C	C#	D♭	D	E♭	E	F	G♭	G	A♭	A	B♭	B	C	D♭	D
F#	G	G#	A	A#	B	B#	C	C#	D	D	D#	E	E#	F#	G	G#	A	A#	B	B#	C#	D	D#
G♭	G	A♭	A	B♭	C♭	B#	C	D♭	D	D	E♭	E	F	G♭	G	A♭	A	B♭	C♭	B#	D♭	D	E♭
G	A♭	A	B♭	B	C	C#	D♭	D	D#	E♭	E	F	F#	G	A♭	A	A#	B	C	C#	D	E♭	E
G#	A	A#	B	B#	C#	D	D	D#	E	E	E#	F#	G	G#	A	A#	B	B#	C#	D	D#	E	E#
A♭	A	B♭	C♭	C	D♭	D	D	E♭	E	F♭	F	G♭	G	A♭	A	B♭	C♭	C	D♭	D	E♭	F♭	F
A	B♭	B	C	C#	D	D#	E♭	E	E#	F	F#	G	G#	A	B♭	B	B#	C#	D	D#	E	F	F#
A#	B	B#	C#	D	D#	E♭	E	E#	F#	F#	G	G#	A	A#	B	B#	C#	D	D#	E	E#	F#	G
B♭	C♭	C	D♭	D	E♭	E	F♭	F	F#	G♭	G	A♭	A	B♭	C♭	C	D♭	D	E♭	E	F	G♭	G
B	C	C#	D	D#	E	E#	F	F#	G	G	G#	A	A#	B	C	C#	D	D#	E	E#	F#	G	G#
	♭2	Maj2	♭3	Maj3	P4	#4	°5	P5	#5	♭6	Maj6	♭7	Maj7	8ve	♭9	Maj9	#9	10	11	#11	12	♭13	13

Fig. 14.4. Interval Cross-Reference Chart

THE CHORD-TONES CROSS-REFERENCE CHART

The Chord-Tones Cross-Reference Chart can be used for testing your chord-tone spelling abilities. As with the Interval Cross-Reference Chart, it works the same as a mileage chart. Find a chord quality in the left column and a root across the top, and then follow the respective row and column to their intersection, which is the spelling for that particular chord.

	C	C♯/D♭	D	E♭	E	F	F♯/G♭	G	G♯/A♭	A	B♭	B
Maj. Triad	C E G	C♯ E♯ G♯ D♭ F A♭	D F♯ A	E♭ G B♭	E G♯ B	F A C	F♯ A♯ C♯ G♭ B♭ D♭	G B D	G♯ B♯ D♯ A♭ C E♭	A C♯ E	B♭ D F	B D♯ F♯
Min. Triad	C E♭ G	C♯ E G♯ D♭ F♭ A♭	D F A	E♭ G♭ B♭	E G B	F A♭ C	F♯ A C♯ G♭ B♭ D♭	G B♭ D	G♯ B D♯ A♭ C♭ E♭	A C E	B♭ D♭ F	B D F♯
Dim. Triad	C E♭ G♭	C♯ E G D♭ F♭ G	D F A♭	E♭ G♭ A	E G B♭	F A♭ C♭	F♯ A C G♭ A C	G B♭ D♭	G♯ B D A♭ C♭ D	A C E♭	B♭ D♭ F♭	B D F
Aug. Triad	C E G♯	C♯ E♯ A D♭ F A	D F♯ A♯	E♭ G B	E G♯ B♯	F A C♯	F♯ A♯ D G♭ B♭ D	G B D♯	G♯ B♯ E A♭ C E	A C♯ E♯	B♭ D F♯	B D♯ G
Maj7	C E G B	C♯ E♯ G♯ C D♭ F A♭ C	D F♯ A C♯	E♭ G B♭ D	E G♯ B D♯	F A C E	F♯ A♯ C♯ E♯ G♭ B♭ D♭ F	G B D F♯	G♯ B♯ D♯ G A♭ C E♭ G	A C♯ E G♯	B♭ D F A	B D♯ F♯ A♯
Maj7(♯5)	C E G♯ B	C♯ E♯ A C D♭ F A C	D F♯ A♯ C♯	E♭ G B D	E G♯ C D♯	F A C♯ E	F♯ A♯ D E♯ G♭ B♭ D F	G B D♯ F♯	G♯ B♯ E G A♭ C E G	A C♯ E♯ G♯	B♭ D F♯ A	B D♯ G A♯
Maj7(♭5)	C E G♭ B	C♯ E♯ G C D♭ F G C	D F♯ A♭ C♯	E♭ G A D	E G♯ B♭ D♯	F A C♭ E	F♯ A♯ C E♯ G♭ B♭ C F	G B D♭ F♯	G♯ B♯ D G A♭ C D G	A C♯ E♭ G♯	B♭ D F♯ A	B D♯ F A♯
Maj6	C E G A	C♯ E♯ G♯ A♯ D♭ F A♭ B♭	D F♯ A B	E♭ G B♭ C	E G♯ B C♯	F A C D	F♯ A♯ C♯ D♯ G♭ B♭ D♭ E♭	G B D E	G♯ B♯ D♯ F A♭ C E♭ F	A C♯ E F♯	B♭ D F G	B D♯ F♯ G♯
7	C E G B♭	C♯ E♯ G♯ B D♭ F A♭ C♭	D F♯ A C	E♭ G B♭ D♭	E G♯ B D	F A C E♭	F♯ A♯ C♯ E G♭ B♭ D♭ F♭	G B D F	G♯ B♯ D♯ F♯ A♭ C E♭ G♭	A C♯ E G	B♭ D F A♭	B D♯ F♯ A
7(♯5)	C E G♯ B♭	C♯ E♯ A B D♭ F A C♭	D F♯ A♯ C	E♭ G B D♭	E G♯ C D	F A C♯ E♭	F♯ A♯ D E G♭ B♭ D F♭	G B D♯ F	G♯ B♯ E F♯ A♭ C E G♭	A C♯ E♯ G	B♭ D F♯ A♭	B D♯ G A
7(♭5)	C E G♭ B♭	C♯ E♯ G B D♭ F G C♭	D F♯ A♭ C	E♭ G A D♭	E G♯ B♭ D	F A C♭ E♭	F♯ A♯ C E G♭ B♭ C F♭	G B D♭ F	G♯ B♯ D♯ F♯ A♭ C D G♭	A C♯ E♭ G	B♭ D F♯ A♭	B D♯ F A
7sus4	C F G B♭	C♯ F♯ G♯ B D♭ G♭ A♭ C♭	D G A C	E♭ A♭ B♭ D♭	E A B D	F B♭ C E♭	F♯ B D♯ E G♭ C♭ D♭ F♭	G C D F	G♯ C♯ D♯ F♯ A♭ D♭ E♭ G♭	A D E G	B♭ E♭ F A♭	B E F♯ A
–7	C E♭ G B♭	C♯ E G♯ B D♭ F♭ A♭ C♭	D F A C	E♭ G♭ B♭ D♭	E G B D	F A♭ C E♭	F♯ A C♯ E G♭ B♭ D♭ F♭	G B♭ D F	G♯ B D♯ F♯ A♭ C♭ E♭ G♭	A C E G	B♭ D♭ F A♭	B D F♯ A
–7(♯5)	C E♭ G♯ B♭	C♯ E A B D♭ F♭ A C♭	D F A♯ C	E♭ G♭ B D♭	E G C D	F A♭ C♯ E♭	F♯ A D E G♭ A D F♭	G B♭ D♯ F	G♯ B E F♯ A♭ C♭ E G♭	A C E♯ G	B♭ D♭ F♯ A♭	B D G A
–Maj7	C E♭ G B	C♯ E G♯ C D♭ F♭ A♭ C	D F A C♯	E♭ G♭ B♭ D	E G B D♯	F A♭ C E	F♯ A C♯ E♯ G♭ A D♭ F	G B♭ D F♯	G♯ B D♯ G A♭ C♭ E♭ G	A C E G♯	B♭ D♭ F A	B D F♯ A♯
–6	C E♭ G A	C♯ E G♯ A♯ D♭ F♭ A♭ B♭	D F A B	E♭ G♭ B♭ C	E G B C♯	F A♭ C D	F♯ A C♯ D♯ G♭ A D♭ E♭	G B♭ D E	G♯ B D♯ F A♭ C♭ E♭ F	A C E F♯	B♭ D♭ F G	B D F♯ G♯
–7(♭5)	C E♭ G♭ B♭	C♯ E G B D♭ F♭ G C♭	D F A♭ C	E♭ G♭ A D♭	E G B♭ D	F A♭ C♭ E♭	F♯ A C E G♭ A C F♭	G B♭ D♭ G	G♯ B D♯ F♯ A♭ C♭ D G♭	A C E♭ G	B♭ D♭ F♭ A♭	B D F A
°7	C E♭ G♭ A	C♯ E G B♭ D♭ F♭ G B♭	D F A♭ B	E♭ G♭ A C	E G B♭ D♭	F A♭ C♭ D	F♯ A C E♭ G♭ A C E♭	G B♭ D♭ E	G♯ B D F A♭ C♭ D F	A C E♭ G♭	B♭ D♭ F♭ G	B D F A♭
°Maj7	C E♭ G♭ B	C♯ E G C D♭ F♭ G C	D F A♭ C♯	E♭ G♭ A D	E G B♭ D♯	F A♭ C♭ E	F♯ A C E♯ G♭ A C F	G B♭ D♭ F♯	G♯ B D G A♭ C♭ D G	A C E♭ G♯	B♭ D♭ F♭ A	B D F A♯
Maj7(9)	C E G B D	C♯ E♯ G♯ C D♯ D♭ F A♭ C E♭	D F♯ A C♯ E	E♭ G B♭ D F	E G♯ B D♯ F♯	F A C E G	F♯ A♯ C♯ E♯ G♯ G♭ B♭ D♭ F A♭	G B D F♯ A	G♯ B♯ D♯ G A♯ A♭ C E♭ G B♭	A C♯ E G♯ B	B♭ D F A C	B D♯ F♯ A♯ C♯
Maj6(9)	C E G A D	C♯ E♯ G♯ A♯ D♯ D♭ F A♭ B♭ E♭	D F♯ A B E	E♭ G B♭ C F	E G♯ B C♯ F♯	F A C D G	F♯ A♯ C♯ D♯ G♯ G♭ B♭ D♭ E♭ A♭	G B D E A	G♯ B♯ D♯ F A♯ A♭ C E♭ F B♭	A C♯ E F♯ B	B♭ D F G C	B D♯ F♯ G♯ C♯
7(9)	C E G B♭ D	C♯ E♯ G♯ C♭ D♯ D♭ F A♭ C♭ E♭	D F♯ A C E	E♭ G B♭ D♭ F	E G♯ B D F♯	F A C E♭ G	F♯ A♯ C♯ E G♯ G♭ B♭ D♭ F♭ A♭	G B D F A	G♯ B♯ D♯ F♯ A♯ A♭ C E♭ G♭ B♭	A C♯ E G B	B♭ D F A♭ C	B D♯ F♯ A C♯
7(♭9)	C E G B♭ D♭	C♯ E♯ G♯ C♭ D D♭ F A♭ C♭ D	D F♯ A C E♭	E♭ G B♭ D♭ E	E G♯ B D F	F A C E♭ G♭	F♯ A♯ C♯ E G G♭ B♭ D♭ F♭ G	G B D F A♭	G♯ B♯ D♯ F♯ A A♭ C E♭ G♭ A	A C♯ E G B♭	B♭ D F A♭ C♭	B D♯ F♯ A C
7(♯9)	C E G B♭ D♯	C♯ E♯ G♯ C♭ E D♭ F A♭ C♭ E	D F♯ A C F	E♭ G B♭ D♭ G♭	E G♯ B D G	F A C E♭ A	F♯ A♯ C♯ E A G♭ B♭ D♭ F♭ A	G B D F A♯	G♯ B♯ D♯ F♯ B A♭ C E♭ G♭ B	A C♯ E G B♯	B♭ D F A♭ C♯	B D♯ F♯ A D
–7(9)	C E♭ G B♭ D	C♯ E G♯ B D♯ D♭ F♭ A♭ C♭ E♭	D F A C E	E♭ G♭ B♭ D♭ F	E G B D F♯	F A♭ C E♭ G	F♯ A C♯ E G♯ G♭ B♭ D♭ F♭ A♭	G B♭ D F A	G♯ B D♯ F♯ A♯ A♭ C♭ E♭ G♭ B♭	A C E G B	B♭ D♭ F A♭ C	B D F♯ A C♯
–Maj7(9)	C E♭ G B D	C♯ E G♯ C D♯ D♭ F♭ A♭ C E♭	D F A C♯ E	E♭ G♭ B♭ D F	E G B D♯ F♯	F A♭ C E G	F♯ A C♯ E♯ G♯ G♭ A D♭ F A♭	G B♭ D F♯ A	G♯ B D♯ G A♯ A♭ C♭ E♭ G B♭	A C E G♯ B	B♭ D♭ F A C	B D F♯ A♯ C♯
–6(9)	C E♭ G A D	C♯ E G♯ A♯ D♯ D♭ F♭ A♭ B♭ E♭	D F A B E	E♭ G♭ B♭ C F	E G B C♯ F♯	F A♭ C D G	F♯ A C♯ D♯ G♯ G♭ A D♭ E♭ A♭	G B♭ D E A	G♯ B D♯ F A♯ A♭ C♭ E♭ F B♭	A C E F♯ B	B♭ D♭ F G C	B D F♯ G♯ C♯
7sus4(9)	C F G B♭ D	C♯ F♯ G♯ B D♯ D♭ G♭ A♭ C♭ E♭	D G A C E	E♭ A♭ B♭ D♭ F	E A B D F♯	F B♭ C E♭ G	F♯ B D♯ E G♯ G♭ C♭ D♭ F♭ A♭	G C D F A	G♯ C♯ D♯ F♯ A♯ A♭ D♭ E♭ G♭ B♭	A D E G B	B♭ E♭ F A♭ C	B E F♯ A C♯
	C	C♯/D♭	D	E♭	E	F	F♯/G♭	G	G♯/A♭	A	B♭	C

Fig. 14.6. Chord Tones Cross-Refence Chart

CHAPTER 15:

POST-CONSTRUCTION PARTY

I would like to thank you for being such a hard worker and getting a great start on your own personal chord dictionary. The search for chords is never ending and much like an adventure game for me. We are fortunate to have the guitar in our lives, and to be able to watch its limitless possibilities roll out before us—if we let them. Stay open to possibilities. We are too young to stop turning over stones to find the treasures beneath.

Good luck, and please let me know how your music is going. Send me some of the chord gems you find.

For a CODA, here is the closing section of a recently written, simple song. It is fun to paint and shade the lyrics with harmonic colors. And as we have discovered, there are plenty to choose from!

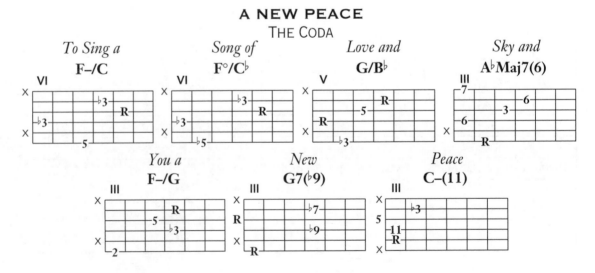

Fig. 15.1. A New Peace

Peace to you!

And to you as well, Jon. I had fun helping out.

Thanks, Chester.

BIBLIOGRAPHY

Persechetti, Vincent. *Twentieth-Century Harmony*. New York: W.W. Norton & Norton, 1961.

American Heritage Dictionary, Third Edition. Boston: Houghton-Mifflin, 1992.

Winchester, Simon. *The Professor and the Madman*. New York: HarperCollins 1998.

Benade, Arthur H. *Horns, Strings, and Harmony*. New York: Dover Publications 1992.

The New Harvard Dictionary of Music. Cambridge: Belknap Press, 1986.

The Groves Dictionary of Music. U.S.A.: Oxford University Press, 2001.

BOOKS FOR DEVELOPING THE "STRUMMING/PLUCKING" COMPING HAND

Faria, Nelson. *The Brazilian Guitar Book*. California: Sher Music Co. 2005. Nelson's book is wonderful for developing a rhythmic vocabulary for Brazilian grooves.

Johnson, Charlton. *Swing and Big Band Guitar*. Hal Leonard Music, 1998. This book focuses on the four-to-the-bar style of Freddie Green.

Giuliani, Mauro. *120 Studies For Right (Plucking) Hand Development*. Alred Publishing Co. 1983. Mauro Giuliani's book is great for finger-style development.

Leavitt, William G. *Melodic Rhythms for Guitar*. Boston: Berklee Press, 2000. William Leavitt's book is wonderful for developing the reading of chord symbols as well as single-note reading.

ABOUT THE AUTHOR

Jon Damian is an active international performer, composer, arranger, lecturer, clinician, and author. He is currently a professor at the Berklee College of Music in Boston. His varied performances have ranged from Luciano Pavarotti to Bill Frisell to Howard McGhee, the Boston Symphony Orchestra under Seiji Ozawa, Johnny Cash, the American Repertory Theater, the Boston Opera Company, the Boston Pops Orchestra, Leonard Bernstein, Jimmy Giuffre, Gunther Schuller, the Bolshoi Ballet, the Boston Ballet, Rosemary Clooney, Linda Ronstadt to Nancy Wilson and Sheila Jordan.

Recordings include the Boston Symphony Orchestra under Seiji Ozawa, Collage, Nova, the *Jazz in the Classroom* series, Bill Frisell, Wolf Soup, the Boston Pops Orchestra, and the Boston Modern Orchestra Project. His recording *Dedications: Faces and Places* with Bill Frisell is now available.

Publications include *The Guitarist's Guide to Composing and Improvising* available through Berklee Press, *A Joyful Noise* available from the CORE Knowledge Foundation, and several articles for *Berklee Today* magazine and *Guitar Player* magazine, and *Heavy Rubber: 30 Years in the Life of An Instrument*, a video documentary about one of Jon Damian's inventions, the Rubbertellie.

Jon Damian is originally from Brooklyn, New York, and some of Jon Damian's private students were Bill Frisell, Wayne Krantz, Kurt Rosenwinkel, Leni Stern, James Valentine, and Mark Whitfield.

Jon Damian uses LaBella strings and Giannini Guitars.

ABOUT CHESTER

Chester is a figment of the imagination and pen of Jon Damian—a foil and imaginary friend created to assist in the extensive detail work and creative exploration involved in building a chord dictionary for the guitar. He can hail from anywhere and be of any age you wish. Most importantly, as Jon says, "It was nice to have Chester around. I couldn't have done it without him!"

More Fine Publications from Berklee Press

GUITAR

BERKLEE BASIC GUITAR
by William Leavitt
Phase 1
50449460 Book Only $9.95
Phase 2
50449470 Book Only $9.95

**CLASSICAL STUDIES
FOR PICK-STYLE GUITAR**
by William Leavitt
50449440 Book $9.95

A MODERN METHOD FOR GUITAR
by William Leavitt
Volume 1: Beginner
50449404 Book/CD $22.95
50449400 Book Only $14.95
Volume 2: Intermediate
50449410 Book Only $14.95
Volume 3: Advanced
50449420 Book $16.95

**A MODERN METHOD
FOR GUITAR 123 COMPLETE**
by William Leavitt
50449468 Book $34.95

MELODIC RHYTHMS FOR GUITAR
by William Leavitt
50449450 Book $14.95

JAZZ IMPROVISATION FOR GUITAR
by Garrison Fewell
50449503 ....$24.95

PLAYING THE CHANGES: GUITAR
By Mitch Seidman
50449509 ....$19.95

VOICE LEADING FOR GUITAR
by John Thomas
50449498 ....$24.95

JIM KELLY GUITAR WORKSHOP SERIES

JIM KELLY'S GUITAR WORKSHOP
00695230 Book/CD $19.95
00320168 DVD/booklet.......................$19.95

MORE GUITAR WORKSHOP
by Jim Kelly
00695306 Book/CD $14.95
00320168 DVD/booklet.......................$19.95

BASS

**CHORD STUDIES
FOR ELECTRIC BASS**
by Rich Appleman
50449750 Book $14.95

INSTANT BASS
by Danny Morris
50449502 Book/CD $14.95

**READING CONTEMPORARY
ELECTRIC BASS**
by Rich Appleman
50449770 Book $19.95

ROCK BASS LINES
by Joe Santerre
50449478 Book/CD $19.95

DRUM SET

BEYOND THE BACKBEAT
by Larry Finn
50449447 Book/CD $19.95

DRUM SET WARM-UPS
by Rod Morgenstein
50449465 Book $12.95

MASTERING THE ART OF BRUSHES
by John Hazilla
50449459 Book/CD $19.95

THE READING DRUMMER
by Dave Vose
50449458 Book $9.95

SAXOPHONE

**CREATIVE READING STUDIES
FOR SAXOPHONE**
by Joseph Viola
50449870 Book $14.95

TECHNIQUE OF THE SAXOPHONE
by Joseph Viola
50449820 Volume 1: Scale Studies $19.95
50449830 Volume 2: Chord Studies $19.95
50449840 Volume 3: Rhythm Studies $19.95

Berklee Press Publications feature material developed at the Berklee College of Music.
To browse the Berklee Press Catalog, go to www.berkleepress.com